Breaking
C *the* • hains

"Only You Can Do It!"

C. S. FLORES

ISBN 978-1-64569-254-6 (paperback)
ISBN 978-1-64569-255-3 (digital)

Christian Faith Publishing, Inc.
832 Park Avenue
Meadville, PA 16335
www.christianfaithpublishing.com

Printed in the United States of America

A life story dedicated to my beautiful mom,
A Rose gone too soon!

Acknowledgments

I would like to thank my charming and witty husband for the sacrifices he makes, his unconditional love, truly caring for our children, and fully supporting me through this venture and being my biggest fan!

To my beautiful children—you are truly God's gift to me. Thank you for believing that God would deliver us and for standing by me through those dark years. I love you guys so dearly!

To my amazing sister, my best friend—you were always there for me during those difficult times. You sustained me in so many ways and never gave up on me.

To my wonderful brother, my caring sister-in-law, my awesome aunt, and my brother-in-law—thank you for your love and support, especially on days when I did not know I needed it.

To *my beautiful* mom—who never got to see my life turn around. Her determination to make her future in the United States of America, paving the way for the rest of our family in this wonderful country, her unconditional love and support in our lives throughout those difficult years, will always remain in our hearts.

To my stepdad—praise God, you and mom now rejoice in Heaven together. Your love and dedication to our mom until the very end could only have been through the LOVE OF GOD in your heart. Your love and support through my darkest hours will always be remembered. Rest in peace.

To the Dawson and Black family—you will always be in our hearts!

Thanks to everyone on my publishing team!

Above all, I want to thank Jesus, my Savior, because without Him, I would not able to do any of this on my own. May my stones of remembrances displaying the power and the amazing love of Jesus Christ be the first step of God's divine purpose in your lives.

CHAPTER 1

As I frantically ran up the stairs of my once-known dream home, the sound of the ringing telephone startled me. Beads of sweat rolled down my forehead as my thumping heart felt like it was about to pop out of my chest. And then I heard his voice! Anger filled the air. Fear immediately took over. Randy was calling from the police station, angrily demanding I come down immediately. On checking the answering machine, he had already left four messages prior. As I looked at the fearful faces of my three beautiful children—Nicole who was then twenty years old, my son Logan who was thirteen years, and little Josiah, five years old—who had no clue what was about to happen, I had to make a decision! Choose to break free or face the deadly consequences that would imprison me for the rest my life! Grabbing my purse and a few items, I frantically dashed for the front door, children in hand, bundling them into the car and driving off into the night.

My story began in April 1979, Junior High, when I met my one and only love and whom my entire world revolved around, Randy Mason—popular, handsome and, not forgetting, a star soccer player for the high school soccer team and the local soccer league. We were high school sweethearts, dating into college years, and then came marriage at the age of twenty-two years.

The terror and imprisonment began during our courtship years, yet I still went ahead, against my dear brother's wishes, and married him. It all started during the school boycott in 1979 which was initiated by the influential music album of Pink Floyd, "Another Brick in the Wall." School back in 1979 was rather peaceful, however, some of the students decided to disrupt classes just for the fun of it. Randy had spotted me on the school grounds gathered around some friends on one of those days, and according to him, he was hooked. Puppy love, I guess! He sent messages through his classmates everyday thereafter, wanting to take me on a date. I had never really dated anyone before, nor did I know anything about dating. Besides, I was rather shy back then too. Randy did not give up, flooding me with messages every day. After two weeks, being influenced by my friends because they thought he was very handsome and he was the most popular boy in the school, I decided to go on a date with him. I had turned away many offers to date before, so he had to be the lucky one, I guess. After three dates, I guess we were officially dating!

Dating the popular boy in school did not prepare me for what was about to come. I suddenly became the envy of many girls in our school. The guys that fancied me were also envious because they had lost their chance of dating me (chuckle). Things were going well until, one day, everything changed. My world was shattered! I never thought that I would be a victim of abuse, besides, back then, abuse of any kind was always kept under wraps. I still remember the first time he struck me, after school at our secret meeting place. I was only trying to find out the truth about him supposedly cheating on me, which later was so true. Ending up with a bust lip was a total shock for me. Seeing my lip bleeding seemed to have scared him, and he apologized for his actions. No one had ever treated me like this before. I should have known then that this would only escalate. But we lived in a closed society back then. Our culture made certain things acceptable, or rather, we thought it is was acceptable, and I was totally naive.

Our dating years were mostly good, but the bad, even though not too often, would override all the good he did do. We went out dancing almost every weekend as we both loved to dance, and we were very good at it. I now became the popular girl at school because I was the star dancer for all the school concerts. Soon, I started to compete in local competitions outside of school. I was also nominated the queen mascot for my brother's local soccer league team. This did not please Randy too much because he did not like the public attention I was getting, and yet, I was innocent and remained loyal to him all the way. Soon, I won my first beauty pageant, and my picture appeared on the front page of the Sunday morning paper. This made Randy very jealous. His mother immediately commented that I was not the right girl her son should be dating. This made Randy even more jealous of me, and he started to grow very possessive in nature. Soon, he insisted on being my dancing partner in all the competitions I participated in. Yet on the other hand, he, too, was the local star of our community because of his soccer talent, and his fame was growing fast.

Dealing with his soccer stardom was not easy. With local fame came the local girls wanting to be with the popular boy. Through those dating years, I should have seen that this relationship was toxic and not of any benefit to me. Looking at those years now proved how ignorant I was back then not to understand or see that being abused was not normal. The apologies after the episodes always seemed sweeter but so downright misleading, yet I could not see beyond what I wanted to see in this relationship.

Remembering this one incident when I became suspicious of Randy's cheating habits, I searched his room and found letters and cards from another girl, which clearly was also his girlfriend with whom he seemed very involved with but secretly. As usual, for fear of Randy, I did not confront him about it. One day, I decided to visit him at his house and confront him with all the letters I found. That was certainly not a good move as that led to a violent confrontation. He began beating me for being inquisitive and invading his privacy as he called it. Wielding a butter knife, threatening to harm me, I still did not think of running away to save myself. I just sat there and took the blows—not one thought of leaving this crazed idiot! Another time, I received a broken nose at my part-time workplace, which should have been a totally embarrassing situation and every reason to break off this relationship, but I didn't. I remained loyal to the one I loved and who I thought loved me. Well, he swore by it that he did.

Randy isolated me from my friends. He would not allow me to go out with them or even talk with them. All telltale signs, and I was completely blinded by "being in love.".

In March 1988, we got married. Our wedding was a glamorous celebration. We had about one thousand guests in attendance. We were excited as we already had our own little place to move into after we got married. On returning from a two-day honeymoon, Randy changed his mind about us living on our own and insisted we move into his parent's house. That was not what I had in mind, and my family was not happy about this. Besides, the house was fully occupied by his other brothers and their wives. Eventually, we got the main floor bedroom. This should have been the first signs of the deadly terror that awaited me, but I did not see it coming.

Having our first child at the age of twenty-three years, dealing with his fame and fortune as he now played professional soccer, with which came drunkenness, late nights out with the team, gambling and, the most feared in all young couples, infidelity! And then behind closed doors, the violence set in as a normal pattern of life. I was alone, confused, and above all, terrified of the only man I loved and who supposedly loved me with all his heart. How could this be!! Too embarrassed to consult with my family, terrified to call the police for help and, most of all, the deadly threats kept me silent.

Living with his family in the family house was no comfort either as I soon found out the other brothers were in the same pattern of life, so to no avail, no help, no comfort. It was clear why Randy saw his abusive ways as normal behavior. He grew up surrounded by this type of behavior. Hence, the brothers behaved in the same way to their wives, and they too accepted this. I could not understand how they would appear to be so courteous to me but could turn violent toward their wives the next minute. It just didn't make any sense, but I was trapped in the same net.

Our living conditions were bad, something that I was not used to. I came from a home with a small family, financially stable, and happy surroundings. My brother was furious, but he did not say anything to me. I guess, he thought I would not pay him any mind. Besides, I was an adult. The fact of the matter was that I was totally naïve.

After six months, opportunity came, and I saw this as a chance to start our lives over. My family was sad that I had to leave my home-town but happy, thinking a new environment meant new changes in our lives, away from the mayhem we were living in. A new start in the big city of Johannesburg, South Africa.

CHAPTER 2

Leaving everything I've ever known and my family, we journeyed to Johannesburg. Nicole was just one month old. We moved in with his older sister to get a start on this new life. Not long after, Randy started a new job and was hired by another professional soccer team. No doubt, his soccer talents never went unnoticed, and he was in great demand by several professional soccer teams. Happiness was short-lived as the old pattern was back—late nights, drinking sprees after the games, and not forgetting the frequent travels to play soccer in other states.

Weekends became a living nightmare when he came home drunk as the beatings started to get violent and more often. Waking up one morning with a visible cut above my swollen nose, his sister flew into a rage. We had one week to find our own apartment as she and Randy got into a big argument. As Nicole turned seven months, I found a job with a local design firm and decided to focus on my career as a fashion designer. For a while, life was peaceful, but the stress of Randy's soccer career, coupled with the drunkenness and more late nights with friends, were becoming unbearable.

A vivid memory of one night as he returned from Cape Town, drunk out of his mind, beating on the door, he stumbled in and all hell broke loose. I would never question Randy about anything because fear gripped me from the outset. Crippled with fear, I would adhere to his every demand just to try to keep the peace, besides, I now had a baby girl that I had to protect from this madness. Stumbling into her room at 1:00 a.m., hanging over her crib, waking up a sleeping baby in his drunken state, trying to carry her and play with her—there was nothing I could do to stop him. And then I saw what I feared the most; he wielded a hunting knife. He grabbed me from behind and, at the same time, hurled threats at me that if ever I tried to take Nicole away from him or if I ever thought of leaving him, he would kill me! I froze in my tracks. For some reason, in his drunken state, he always imagined I was fighting back, and he would get more angry. The terror kept me silent. As he staggered around with me in a chokehold, the knife nicked me on my left arm. The sight of my bleeding arm did not deter him to stop. Punches and blows I remembered so vividly, and all I could do was shield my face from the blows as I had to be at work the next day. How would I explain the bruises? Besides, that would be more of an embarrassment, or so I thought back then. This was a living nightmare that played over and over and over again. Weekends became something I dreaded.

Days turned into weeks, into months, into years; all the same things just got worse. The strangest thing was that there were days when everything was so peaceful, and we seemed happy that I almost couldn't believe that this was the same person I was married to. The case of Dr. Jekyll and Hyde would be the best way to describe the situation, I guess.

One evening, a knock on our apartment door was about to alter our lives drastically. Standing at the door was a fellow teammate and his mother whom I have never met. With no clue that my life was about to spiral even further out of control, as I lay two-year-old Nicole down for her evening nap, the muffled conversation in the living room got louder and more agitated. On entering the living room, the words that I heard was like a knife cutting right through my heart

"My daughter is pregnant, and what are you going to do about it?" Eyes brimming with tears, I was forced to hold my composure in a civilized manner. Even if I tried to say something, there were no words coming out of my mouth. Call it a state of shock or maybe anger; I could not tell! As Randy shut the door behind him after our so-called "uninvited guests" took their leave, he turned around to start explaining. I exploded into a rage like never before. If there was any time for an opportunity to leave this horrid life, this would have been the day. For the first time, I held the cards of play in my hands. Hysterically, I ordered Randy to get out of our apartment, but he refused to leave. For the first time, he was begging for a chance, knowing that our marriage could end, and he would lose his precious daughter—or so I thought. For weeks, there was no conversation in our household. Randy "tiptoed" around me, while I had retreated into total silence, no way to share with anyone what I was going through. How could I? A total embarrassment this was!

A couple months later, Randy was summoned to court to face a judge concerning paternity and possible child support. This was the first time I realized that he was so afraid of the law. He begged me to accompany him to the courts, and only God knows why I ever agreed to do so. Coming face to face with the person that was partially responsible for destroying our home was gut wrenching. Anger flared up inside of me, yet there was a part of me that felt pity for her. The results of the tests proved he was guilty as charged. Yet another opportunity to end this nightmare of a marriage, but I did not. Why? I just didn't know. Things were never the same after all this. But life continued. The beatings had stopped, and Randy was trying very hard to win my heart back. I saw this as my chance to give him a choice in life. Randy had to choose between having a family and keeping our marriage or continue to follow his professional soccer career. Although trying to do that would be difficult because this was his teammate's sister after all.

CHAPTER

A year passed, and everything was smooth, and we were getting ready to move into our first home. Sounds absolutely crazy, but I did choose to give our marriage another chance. Part of my culture, I guess. One month after moving into our new home, the sound of the intercom late one night turned everything upside down—again! It seemed that peace was far from our lives, more like not meant for us. Randy's teammate's mother found out our whereabouts and was at the gate yelling and threatened to bring in the police if he did not acknowledge his infidelity! Randy somehow convinced her to leave.

The next day, I packed a bag, picked up Nicole from daycare, and left to fly home to my brother's house, in my hometown. I had taken just about all my mind could absorb at the time, too exhausted for any more confrontations. Two days later, Randy showed up. Now being on familiar ground and away from all the drama happening in Johannesburg, he felt he was in charge again. The drinking spree started, which obviously was his way to get me into fear mode, and he knew he would succeed. Randy, like most people, thought that alcohol could solve problems, so he indulged. Here I was, too embarrassed and scared to tell my family what had transpired. I tried to play the whole situation off.

Unbeknownst to me, my brother had somehow found out about Randy's escapade. Filled with rage, he did not allow Randy into his home. And then tempers flared up. Now bearing in mind, at this stage in my life, I had not met my Savior Jesus yet. All I had as a refuge were my Indian Hindu gods in which I thought I found comfort, but to no avail! Randy's rage exploded, and there was no holding him back. My brother who is the calmest and most loving of all people, flew into a rage. I had never seen him like that before. There was no way he was going to stand for anybody mistreating or disrespecting his baby sister, let alone in his presence! One sturdy punch, and Randy was thrown to the ground. Staggering in his drunkenness, cursing, and yelling, it stirred up the fear in me, and I knew, if I did not leave with him, it would only get worse even though I was aware what awaited me after all of this! To avoid further disruption and trying to protect my little Nicole from seeing all of this, reluctantly, I left my safety zone and went with Randy, fully knowing what awaited me.

No sooner had I jumped into the car that the beatings began as he tried to steer the vehicle at the same time. Yes, utter madness, which did not make any sense at the time. I was in a position all too familiar. The next two days, we spent at his parent's home, which was of no refuge or comfort to me either. However, the only person he had some respect for was his father who, somehow, over the years, got to love and care for me rather deeply. He spoke with Randy and tried to show him that it was wrong to behave in that manner. Randy, as always, promised never to lay his hands on me again. That was my saving grace. For now, at least.

By this time, the anger inside of me began turning into dislike—dislike which I could never display or make verbal. I was so wrapped up in disliking Randy for who he was that any good he tried to do I never saw it as good. Even when he tried to love me, it did not feel real to me. It had been two months since we had returned to Johannesburg, and I had no contact with any members of my family since the last episode that transpired at my brother's house. By this time, Randy got hooked onto horse racing, and gambling began to find its place in our home and our already dying marriage.

Now money became the prime focus of our already struggling battles. Randy was gambling his entire paycheck every month and had now started to dip into my paycheck. At first, it was just a couple of hundred dollars (rands for South African currency). Not long, it was my entire paycheck, and if I refuse to give it when he would ask, then the never-ending nightmare would begin. By this time, Nicole was three years old and was beginning to understand things, and the violent disruptions disturbed her tremendously. The strange thing was, he would try to console her with such love and care. I could almost say this must have really caused a lot of confusion in Nicole's mind. How could her daddy love her and be so tender and yet, be violent and mistreat her mom on the other hand.

Within months of moving in, we were facing pre-foreclosure! The obvious reason was Randy was not paying the mortgage, and I had no clue until it was too late. Having consulted with the bank manager, I managed to negotiate a deal and the house was put up for sale and the full outstanding amount was recovered. What a relief that was for me.

Once again, we had to pick up and move. This time, back to the city center of Johannesburg. I had no clue at this very time Randy was also bracing to lose his top paying job at ACE Laboratories for not showing up to work regularly as the gambling losses led to further drinking, causing him not to be able to attend work. And so here we were again, on a downward spiral in life. Luckily, I still held my job, and no matter what I had gone through the night before, I was showing up to work the next day with this horrendous secret.

Five months later, we decided to move to a suburb close to the city as Nicole was almost kindergarten age and would need to attend school soon. Life was peaceful and excitement set in as we moved into another phase of our lives—again, thinking a change of place would mean a change of life. The drinking and gambling seemed to have halted. I still sought my solace in my Hindu gods, daily praying they would bring the peace I needed and fill the void in my heart. Yet again, to no avail. By this time, I had found a nanny for Nicole as it was imperative I keep my job if we wanted to survive in this big city.

For a while, life seemed to follow a normal pattern like a normal family. We began to thrive and success seemed inevitable. Everything was fantastic. Weekends away, bought a new car, a red VW Jetta,

I remember—life seemed good. Randy had now started a new job with his younger sister who lived next door with her own family—another good paying job with higher position than the last job. You see, Randy worked in accounts, and he was pretty good at it. Now he had a good chance of making it to become a chartered accountant. With all of this supposedly good fortune, the discussion of having another baby popped up. Call me crazy, but here I was with someone I didn't really want to be with, someone that I feared, and now I'm thinking of having another baby? I GUESS MY MIND HAD TO HAVE BEEN REALLY TWISTED!

You see, the thing was, after we would go through our turbulent episodes, Randy would swear he loved me with all his heart, yet he never apologized for his behavior the night before. I guess this must have played with my emotions, and I always hoped he would change for the good. I have seen many friends that were transformed from bad to being good; I guess that always left me hoping for the best in my marriage. But I never, for once, recognized that these were signs of domestic abuse. Anyway, two months after that discussion, BABY BOOM! I was pregnant with our second child. I still remember the day I got the news how excited I was, couldn't wait to get home to tell Randy. For a while, the household was joyous and full of baby talk; everything seemed to be going as planned.

As always, earning good money was wonderful BUT with it came the temptation—horse racing and, this time, casino fever!! This time, seven times worse than before. And then it happened—again. One morning, Randy attempted to get money from me, and I would not give in. Being five months pregnant, you would have thought that would stop him. How wrong was I! What was I thinking having another child be exposed to this! Trying to protect my bulging belly, I took the incoming blows to my already hurting back and to my head. Grabbing me by my long hair, he threw me onto the bed, and there was no escaping what came next.

Life took on its old pattern and seemed endless. I was struggling with bills on my own because Randy spent his monthly paycheck on the races and casinos. The only good thing at the time was the medical insurance we had. We had 100 percent coverage as this was being deducted from his monthly salary, so all my medical expenses were fully covered. As I closed on my eighth month of pregnancy, once again. we were in a deep dark hole. I found myself having to sell our furniture and appliances to cover Randy's gambling debts, yet it was not enough to cover the last month's rent. Then the strangest thing happened. Randy had run into an old friend from the south coast city where we both grew up. He invited us over to his home for lunch one weekend. I was so taken aback by the beautiful homes I saw. My dream to own one of these was one of my long deep desires. The afternoon reunion and conversation ended in us finding a home for lease for almost half the cost we were paying in the city suburbs. So the logical thing to do was move—again—just like all the other times, thinking a new place will bring peace and yet another chance for our marriage. I have to say, my Jesus, although I was far from any knowledge of Him, had to be watching over me each time I had to give up our home, and the landlords always granted me favor and let me out of the leases with no consequences.

CHAPTER 4

So here we were, in a new beautiful three-bedroom, two-bathroom home with a gigantic pool in the back yard, fully secured. Now back in the day, home security was very necessary as every area had its crime, and this would be a precaution. One habit that I had was to always pray before entering a new home, and here I was with my Hindu gods, again thinking that they would deliver me from my nightmarish life. Little did I know that this would be the home where I would meet my Jesus, my Lord, my Savior, coming to my rescue.

As the month of April 1994 approached, South Africa was also getting ready to make history. Nelson Mandela was released from prison after twenty-seven years and was campaigning for president. It was a no brainer back then that he was going to win due to the enormous black vote majority. And he did.

Randy's younger sister also decided to move into the same neighborhood. Since she bought all new furniture, we took her hand me downs as most of our furniture were sold to cover the debts we had accumulated. Time had come to deliver my baby. A one-hour trek to the city hospital and not long afterwards, a beautiful baby boy was born! With some complications, he was delivered via caesarean section but healthy and beautiful. Having a male child is always a big celebration as he will carry the father's last name! A celebration it was, even with receiving a two hundred and fifty rand (South African currency) parking violation as Randy was so excited, he parked in a no-parking-zone spot.

Later that evening, he brought Nicole to meet her new baby brother for the first time. Nicole saw her baby brother, Logan, and the first words that came out her mouth were, "Why is he so dark in complexion?" Now Miss Nicole was born very light skinned, with beautiful black hair like my grandma, so who was this little dark-skinned baby? That remained a family joke for many years.

Seven days in the hospital, and now it was time to go home and start another chapter in our lives. To my surprise, my sister-in-law (my brother's wife, who was mom for me for the longest time as my mom had emigrated to the United States many years prior) and a family friend were at my home to welcome me and the new addition. Few days had passed, and then another big surprise. My mom showed up from Miami, unexpectedly, to visit. Little did I realize that my mom would be the link between me and meeting my Jesus.

I was in a lot of pain due to the C-section that I had, and it seemed that I was not getting any better. My mom had seen the sadness in my eyes for the first time. It broke her heart. As a mother, she sensed a lot more was wrong with this marriage and our home. Now at the same time, Randy's mother showed up to see her new grandson. Randy, on the other hand, was celebrating, drunk every day from the time I got home from the hospital.

Now winter was setting in in Johannesburg, and the cold was extreme. This house, as beautiful as it looked, was not equipped to embrace the severely cold weather. You see, in South Africa, air conditioners were not a common item. If it was hot, you used a fan and opened your doors and windows; in the winter, we used space heaters. Having in laws under the same roof was not a good idea. Here was my mom, ultra-modern and way ahead of her time, and then there was my mother-in-law, a typical Indian Hindu woman, totally old school. They were courteous though to each other while in each other's company. By the end of that evening, she insisted Randy drive her back to the south coast city, which was a six-hour journey by car. My mom was astounded when he willingly agreed to take her, without giving a second thought about me or the children. In reality, if my mom and sister-in-law had not come by, I would have been left alone to manage with the new baby and a now four-year-old Nicole. But little did we know that God was orchestrating all of this so he could make his move.

That Sunday, my mom and Nicole went to church with my friend and his wife. They attended this little church which was held in the local elementary school, Faith Fellowship. My mom had remained with me for the next two months of her stay in South Africa. Randy returned home after a week in the south coast. My mom and him reconnected on his return, and all seemed to be fine. One Sunday, while Randy was away playing soccer, my mom and Nicole went to church as they normally did. All I remember was my mom returning that afternoon with my friend, who was now a deacon, and the pastor of Faith Fellowship, Pastor Joseph.

I will never forget that Sunday afternoon. David and Pastor Joseph started to pray over me and something strange happened. First, all the pain I was experiencing lifted from my belly. With my eyes closed, I felt this warm sensation over my body, and I felt like I was running free in the meadows with all this white light surrounding me. I never felt so free in my entire life. When they were done, I felt like a different person—like a burden had been lifted off my shoulders. I was smiling for absolutely no reason at all; call me crazy. And then Pastor Joseph and David asked the question, "Would you like to give your heart to Jesus?"

Now, I knew the name Jesus very well as I grew up among other Christians, but I did not know Him! Without hesitation, I said, "Yes."

I had no clue what had just happened except that I felt better, and I was not the same person that I was a week ago. Now that I made this commitment, the next step was no easy task as I was dedicated to the Hindu gods prior to me giving my heart to the Lord. The ties had to be broken completely. The idols had to be removed from my home, the ceremonial yellow string with the gold idol nuggets which was tied during my Hindu marriage vows had to be removed from my neck and all destroyed. Now it is true that once you make a commitment to follow Jesus, all is forgiven and you are free, but in this case, the idols had to be destroyed to sever all ties permanently.

When Randy got back home later that afternoon, I told him what had transpired, and in a few days, the idols were to be removed from our home, and the matrimonial string was be removed and destroyed. Now just to understand this, the matrimonial string, coupled with the red dot on my forehead which I religiously wore daily, meant that I was a married Hindu woman. Discarding these things, for a Hindu woman, would indicate the marriage has ended. So out of respect for Randy, the Pastor had to ask if that would be something Randy would agree to. Now I did say that God was already in charge and orchestrating all moves. To everyone's surprise, he said yes without hesitation. And so, it was done. For the next three months, it was attending church in the tiny classroom every Sunday and Tuesday night. Both Nicole and Logan were dedicated to the Lord. After attending a few baptisms, Pastor Joseph felt I was ready for the next step. November 1994 of the same year, I got baptized, and the following month, to my surprise, so did Randy. And here we were, a brand-new family in Christ, making all things new, with the old buried away. Life was real and different for the first time.

Four months passed, and this dark cloud loomed over us. Randy got fired from his job, only to find out he had stolen money from the company to feed his gambling spree, which he had started again without my knowledge. Afraid he may be sent to jail, he picked up and left to go home to "mommy" in the south coast. Left with two young children, no income, and with a gambling debt over my head, I had to find a way to solve this mess, just like I always got him out of the messes he made. Now being the fact that he left me, it could have been a break to get away from him and end this marriage. I was still on maternity leave. I could have gone back to work and continued to make my life in Johannesburg. But being a new Christian, I was thinking I was doing the right thing by tying up all our business in Johannesburg and following after him. I was new to the Christian faith. I had not yet learned the power of God's Word or how to apply it to my life. I could not share my troubled situation with my pastor either. I was too embarrassed and very afraid of Randy to do so. My uncle owned a furniture transport business, and he volunteered to move my remaining furniture and store it in his warehouse.

CHAPTER 5

On my arrival in the south coast, the only place I could stay was at my sister's place. Bridges were already burnt with my brother from the last episode with Randy. He was not angry with me, but he and Randy were not on speaking terms. I avoided all conversation with my brother for the fear of having to face making that dreadful decision, which I knew I couldn't make because I feared Randy so much.

So here I was, with two children, no job, no money, inconveniencing my sister who herself was not in a good state with her marriage, and the fact that she had a tiny two-bedroom home. However, she welcomed me and the kids. And my brother-in-law, being Randy's best mate, invited him over to stay as well. The first week of our stay was horrendous as now Randy had a drinking mate—my brother-in-law. Now bearing in mind, my sister was going through a similar situation I was in but with three children in tow. All the children slept in one of the bedrooms, while Randy and I slept in the tiny living room on the floor.

This arrangement continued for two months until, one day, my brother-in-law and my sister got into a violent argument. He, too, was quick tempered, on one hand, and could be so loving and entertaining on the other. Another case of Dr. Jekyll and Hyde. Tempers were rising between Randy and my brother-in-law, and Randy lunged forward and held him back to restrain him from striking my sister again. In spite of all that Randy had put me through, he loved my sister very dearly and was not going to tolerate her being disrespected or abused. How crazy was all of this because, here he was, doing the same thing to me, yet he could not tolerate someone else being abused. I guess, you can call it ignorance!

Randy withdrew from my brother-in-law's company and now realized that this was no way to live. Living there became very uneasy and strained. By this time, my sister had already made up her mind to leave her nineteen-year marriage and head for the United States where my mom lived. The plan was, I return to Johannesburg and prepare a place for her and the kids, and she would come over and prepare her escape to the US. And so it was.

Randy and I, with our two children, left for Johannesburg one morning. Now I had sought refuge with one of my Christian friends. Maggie and Mark had five children and lived in a three-bedroom home. Now when I look at this situation, I saw how the hand of God was at work. Maggie and Mark were our mentors in our new Christian walk. They also attended Faith Fellowship. Now it was seven children and four adults in one household, with only Mark who had a job. If this was not the hand of God at work, then I don't know what to call this.

This was a time of daily fellowship and blessing and a living testimony of what the Lord can do in the lives of Christians. Our fellow brothers and sisters in Christ saw the work the Lord was doing in all our lives. Randy soon got a new job, and after the first month, we were able to find a house down the street from Maggie and Mark. My uncle had transported our furniture back to Johannesburg to our new house. The presence of the Lord filled our home. We were attending church full time and the blessing of the Lord was in abundance. I became a full-time stay-at-home mom for the next two years. Life was a bliss especially with the Lord being the center of our household. Randy became the church transporter driving the church bus.

A month later, my sister had escaped from the south coast city in secret with the kids as she planned so she could make her move to the United States. Preparations had to be made quickly and secretly as my brother-in-law was now searching for my sister and the kids.

Discovering their whereabouts would have deadly consequences for my sister. She now realized, if she wanted to escape this life and be successful, she really needed to do this. Besides, she would be giving her kids a chance at a better future. Within four weeks of her arrival, my sister was on her way to the United States of America, SAFE AND SOUND!

You would think, by now, this would have given me some food for thought too, right? But I guess, I was not thinking of it because everything was going smoothly, especially now that we were serving the Lord. Oh yes, not long after, I discovered that Randy was having an affair with my friend's niece. How embarrassing. She accommodated us when we did not have a place to stay, and this is the way to repay her kindness? Then the girl had the nerve to show up at my door because her father now put her out and thinking that I was not aware of the affair. But I did the Christian thing and allowed her in but told Randy that he needed to get her out immediately, and at the same time, I made him aware that I was very well aware of what was going on between them. She pleaded with me not to put Randy out as there was no longer anything between them, and she apologized profusely for her misjudgment, asking for forgiveness. I remained silent.

For months, things were very mellow in our home, but church was still a priority. Two months, later, Randy's younger brother showed up at our door. His wife and him had split up, and he chose to head for Johannesburg. I did not fancy this idea because Randy was easily influenced by him. There was no drinking of alcohol or smoking in our home. I asked his brother to please adhere and respect our home while he was there. I knew this was not a good idea, but I did the Christian thing and allowed him to stay. One morning, while praying, the Lord showed me this scripture from Mark 3:25, "A house divided against itself cannot stand." I knew immediately his brother had to leave. I could sense trouble coming. That Sunday, I invited him to church as I was going to sing my testimony song to the congregation. He was so touched by the song and the message that day that he started to consider who this Jesus Christ was. A seed was planted that day. A few days later, he came home drunk, and I did not fancy that at all. I knew, if he continued to stay, it would not be long before Randy would be doing the same thing, and that would brood a whole lot of new trials for us. I had to ask his brother to leave my home, and surprisingly, Randy agreed that it was the right thing to do.

CHAPTER

At the end of the first year, we were given first choice to purchase this home we were living in. So we applied for a mortgage, but a cash buyer superseded our offer, and we had two months to move out. Fortunately, the house across the street was being leased, and we got first preference. Here we were again, another move. Within a month of moving in, I started a job. Nicole was in elementary school down the street, and Logan was just two years old now. I managed to find a trustworthy nanny for the kids and tried to settle into a normal pattern of life.

Now it had been more than a year since Randy had laid his hands on me, so everything seemed to be cordial. Randy used a car-pool to go to his job, and I got to use the new car we acquired. Until, one day, Randy decided to drop me off at work and use our car. At first, I didn't think anything about it, but slowly, he started to skip days off from work, be late in picking me up, leave at strange hours to go see friends. And then I thought, *Hmm, something doesn't feel right here.*

Seeking the Lord diligently daily, I sought wisdom and guidance. I didn't want to upset the apple cart, as you would call it, as I had to be absolutely certain I was on the right track. Taking into account that I'm not in the wrong, I was still fearful that if Randy found me snooping around, that would be a cause to stir up anger, and I very well knew where that anger would lead. I was searching the car for evidence, going through his pockets, just trying to find something to give me a lead. Months went by, and nothing. Before long, Randy lost his job and yet, he was still dropping me off at work every day. And then one day, a breakthrough. It was like God had wanted me to be right there where I needed to be. I was in the bathroom, and I heard a muffled voice outside the window. Randy was on his cell phone talking to someone. I will never forget the words that I heard, how deep it cut into my heart, ripping it out into pieces: "I do love you very much too! I can't wait to see you tonight!"

You cannot imagine the thoughts and feelings that went through me at that very moment! *How dare he do this again!* I confronted him when he came inside, and the calm response, I received was that he was on the phone with his male friend Danny. After all the years of putting up with his infidelity, I had to be smart dealing with Randy always getting over me with the things he did. I did not disclose at the time that I overheard the actual conversation. My thing was now to get hold of the phone number that he had been calling ever so often.

So the next day, I pretended that I was going to work. Actually, I got a ride with his friend Danny as we worked in the same place. At about 10:00 a.m., I told Danny I needed to go home urgently. On our way, I disclosed to Danny what had transpired, and I was going to catch Randy red-handed. I made Danny park a little way down from where I could see our home over the wall. And there was Randy, standing at the doorway smoking a cigarette. I could not see anyone else. Within a few minutes, Randy jumped into our car and headed to the local shopping center, pulled up, and there I saw what most women would dread to see—a young girl in her school uniform getting into the car. Unfortunately, Danny was reluctant to follow them as he did not want to be involved in this matter, or did he actually know about this and just felt guilty for not telling me he knew. I chose to respect his wishes, but that did not stop me from wanting to catch Randy red-handed.

A few days later, our car got repossessed due to nonpayment on the loan. It had been months since Randy had made any payments because, by this time, he had lost yet another job. How I was able to be silent through all of this could only be the grace of the Lord upon me. One morning, I got up and decided I was going to follow Randy—on foot! As he walked off, a few minutes later, I dashed off after him. We must have walked at least two miles, maybe more, before I saw him approach a house and enter. Nervous as I was and more afraid of being caught following him, I hid behind a wall and waited. The heat was blazing down as this was in the summer, and the summers could be brutal in the day. There he was getting into another car.

As he pulled out the driveway, it was like something inside me snapped. The next thing I knew, I was alongside the car, my hands grabbing onto his shirt through the open window, yelling at him furiously as he tried to drive off. The fear on the face of the young girl was of pure shock as Randy managed to drive off. I would never forget the look on Randy's face that day—absolute shock and maybe a little terrified—terrified that he was actually caught red-handed by me. Now I knew all too well what was to happen next. I knew for a fact that Randy was infuriated and probably embarrassed because I had caught him red-handed once and for all. Having a moment to realize what had just happened, fear welled up inside of me because I knew what awaited me once Randy got his hands on me.

Scared to death, I rushed to the neighbor's house and knocked on the door. I quickly explained what had just transpired, and she willingly let me in. I asked if she knew the young girl, and it so happened the girl was her cousin. Compassion filled the lady's heart, and she was so sorry that all of this was happening to me. We spoke for a few hours, and I knew Randy would be frantically searching for me now. Moments later, we saw Randy ride by her house, and he had my baby boy with him. Now I knew I was in real trouble. How do I go home, well knowing what awaited me? Eventually, after two hours, I headed back home and hid in the bathroom. I told my nanny to please make sure that the children were safe and fed, and I told her what just happened, only to find out that she already knew about Randy's affair but was afraid of saying anything for fear of losing her job.

Randy had been bringing this young girl, sixteen years of age, to our home during the day and having sex with her in our own bed; how disgusting! He was a thirty-five-year-old man! As the evening closed in, I had no choice but to come out of my hiding place and face the consequences. What a night of terror it was. Where was my God? Kicks and blows flew as I took the strikes from a broomstick to my head and body, just trying to shield my face. Why was my God allowing this happen to me? Battered and bruised, he locked me out the house that night. I stood in the cold, crying out silently to my Lord, why had he forsaken me!

Days passed, and there was no conversation. The atmosphere remained as cold as ice. Avoiding him at all costs if I could, I carried out my motherly duties. Months passed, and Randy thought everything was back to normal, or at least, I made him think that. By this time, I was not working anymore, and Randy had partnered with a friend in a car dealership business, or so I thought. In reality, his friend was involved in car thefts, skimming off VIN numbers, and reselling these cars across the border. Oh yes, now Randy was in the big time, or so he thought. But it was paying the bills for now, a roof over our heads, and food to eat. But yet, he did not give up on the relationship with the girl.

So yet another day, I followed him and, this time, to Danny's house. I hid behind a shrub and waited for him. Hours passed, and he emerged from the house only to be greeted by me at door. The shock of seeing me at the door and now knowing that I am fully aware of his affair with this girl caused him to fly into a horrendous rage. I remember him grabbing me by my throat and pulling me into the house. As I started asking questions, he began to punch and kick me furiously. In the meantime, the girl was in the other room listening to this commotion. Whether she knew this was his type of behavior I had no idea, but at least, now she knew the type of person he was. I clearly remember him dragging me outside and throwing me against his friend's car. My face went smack against the side mirror of the car. By this time, his rage was out of control. He grabbed hold of my hair with one hand and punched me with the other. He shoved me into the car and drove me home, where the drama continued. Behind closed doors, the beatings continued. Fortunately, Nicole was still at school, and my nanny grabbed Logan and took him to her living quarters at the back of the house. She was good at protecting him that way. God bless her heart.

By the time Randy was done, I lay on the floor writhing in pain. Every part of my body ached so bad. My head felt like it was on fire and about to burst. Slowly, I managed to lift myself off the floor and headed to the bathroom. As I looked into the mirror, I gasped! *Who was this person in the mirror?* Totally unrecognizable! Bruises and swelling puffed out my face, my eyes barely open, my arms scratched and badly bruised, don't even mention my body, black and blue all over. My spine felt as though it was on fire! The pain travelled through like a bolt of lightning from top to bottom. *Where was my Jesus?* I thought. I must have done something to upset the Lord for Him to forsake me like this! I slowly made my way to the guest room where I locked myself in as I did not want the kids to see me like this. My nanny, Cindy, was truly a blessing. She ensured that the kids were taken care of. Two days I remained in the room, refusing any meals, abstaining from any conversation. Randy walked in when I unlocked the door for Cindy to bring me some water so I could take some pain pills to ease my pain. He just stood there and looked at me, no expression on his face. He turned and walked right out. By the time the third day came, I was overwhelmed with emotion, pain, and distress. Once again, all alone and no one to share this with, except a gruesome visual reminder and the emotional reminder of being threatened with death by Randy if I ever called the police or my family.

I looked into the mirror that morning of the third day and knew I had to end this. There was no more of this I could take. There was only one way out! Yes, one way only. Hands trembling, I opened the bathroom cabinet and, therein, lay my answer to end all pain and suffering once and for all. I cannot remember how many pills I swallowed, but all I saw was the end to this madness. Within a few minutes, I staggered back to my room only to collapse on the floor. And then it hit me. What have I done! How can I leave my poor innocent children with a monster like him? Obviously, the kids did not know everything about their father except that he loved them. They were too young to understand all that was going on. Completely disorientated, I dragged myself to the open window and began calling out to Cindy for help. I guess, Jesus really was on my side and was with me at that moment as, by some miracle, she heard me and came running to my aid. She dragged me into the bathroom and immediately tried to induce me to vomit. There was no way to call the emergency crisis line as we did not have a land line or another cell phone. Then it was a matter to explain why I tried to overdose. Eventually, Cindy succeeded. She stayed by my bedside for the rest of the afternoon, making sure that I was going to be okay. She took complete control of the household for that week.

As for Randy, still no reaction. He was in and out of the house as usual as though nothing was wrong. That Sunday, David and wife, my friends from church, showed up. I was lying down, and Cindy showed them to my room. Most of the swelling had gone down, but the bruises were still quite evident. Being shocked was the last thing I expected from them. David's wife just hugged me and told me that Jesus loves me no matter what. "By His stripes we are healed." David just stood at the doorway, tears rolling down his face. Not much was discussed that night, but praying in the spirit we did. Jesus was with me, after all, even through all that beating.

CHAPTER

Months passed by, and there was no change. Our home became a silent hellhole. Until one evening, there was a heavy booming knock on the door. Randy opened the door, and to his big surprise, there at the doorway was standing this young girl with both her parents raging in anger. Politely, they asked to be invited in. What an awkward moment this was.

The father of the girl angrily asked the girl, who was now a nervous wreck, to apologize to me for all the trouble she had caused. Her parents did not realize that Randy was a thirty-six-year-old married man with two children, but I guess on finding out, that brought them to our doorstep that night. And so the angry conversation began. Randy had led them and the girl to believe that he was twenty-one years old. Come to find out that Randy had also promised this girl divorce papers for her upcoming seventeenth birthday, which was in a few weeks.

Randy was now also nervous because he never thought that he would get caught in this illicit affair, but moreover, he was afraid that the girl's father would call the police. He confessed to the father that was true but had no intentions of proceeding with it. Randy leave his wife? No way! Life would be a mess because there would be no one to clean up his messes or take the fall for his weaknesses. Besides, then everybody would come to know about this embarrassing situation.

Randy never, in his wildest dreams, thought that he would get caught out.

In all of this, I just burst out in anger and told the girl she can take him right now because I don't want him anymore. Head down and crying, with remorse or fear, I couldn't tell, she refused. She announced that she did not want to have anything more to do with him. The father assured me that his daughter will no longer cause me any more trouble. As they stepped outside, Randy. the coward he was, started cursing at the girl and calling her all sorts of vicious names, and that was for turning him down and laying all the blame on him. I now know for a fact, if it wasn't for them seeing our two innocent children, Randy would have been in jail for statutory rape even though this affair was consensual.

Weeks turned into months, and there was still not much conversation in our home. By this time, money had begun to run low, and things were getting really difficult. I was unable to get a job as transportation became a big issue. The city was one hour away from this town, and no bus service was available. That was the first time the thought of going to the United States to join my mom and sister crossed my mind. Every day, I watched the airplanes fly across the skies and would pray that, someday, it will be my kids and I on that plane—someday!

Not long after that, the illegal car business was uncovered, and law enforcement was crawling all over his friend's business, only to also uncover that Randy was involved in credit card fraud as well. He had gotten involved with the wrong crowd this time, one of Johannesburg's most notorious criminals. Unbeknownst to me, law enforcement had already caught Randy on a sting operation a few days ago, and for immunity, had to testify against those involved. He had no clue who he was involved with. Giving part of the syndicate up to the police that night caused all hell to break loose. Randy pitched up at home that night and hurriedly packed a bag saying that he was in some kind of trouble and was headed for the south coast city for safety, and he was taking with him my baby boy who was now four years old. Leaving Nicole and I behind, we had no clue what we were about to face that night.

He left, gone without a trace, and I had no knowledge of all that had transpired earlier on that evening. At 1:00 a.m., there was a loud noise outside, and I heard shuffling noises. Burglary was a common trend at that time in the area where we lived, so my first reaction was to peek through the curtains to see. No sooner than movement was detected inside the house, the banging on the door startled us, and shouting that it was the police. But once again, God was with us and never let up. I grabbed my Nicky and hid her in the closet. Bewildered with all the commotion outside, I heard angry voices planning to break down the door, but they would have to get through the heavy barricaded security gate first. That's when I realized that this was no the police but the gang members looking for Randy. If ever I cried out to God, it was that night, for strength and protection—Psalm 91.

After several minutes of them trying to break through, I set off the burglar alarm to deter them. The alarm services to the local police was disconnected, but at least, that would deter them. In Johannesburg, very rarely would the neighbors come out at night in cases like this for the fear of their own families and the known fact that they never knew the type of weapons the perpetrators may be carrying. I waited until first light and ran over to my neighbor's house to call Randy to tell him what we have been through that night. And his response, "Why did you not call the police?" How? No phone in our home. Danger outside. Risk my life and my daughter's for something he did! On top of all this, Randy had stolen some of my neighbor's art which she had stored in our garage. She was livid when she found out and did not believe that I had no part in that, nor did I know that he had taken it and sold it.

This was it for me! I had to get out and get out now! I found myself a job and moved back into the city center with Nicole. The company I worked for rented apartments in the city, and I was so blessed that one was available right on time. With David's help, I moved in with the little possessions I had left. Starting over didn't matter as long as Nicky and I were safe. Four months passed, and my phone rang one day. Randy was on the other end of the line. I presumed his sister must have given him my contact details as I had to keep up with my baby boy's welfare who I had not seen in over four months. He heard that I had settled in and was working again.

This was my weakness every time. I allowed him back into my life, besides, that was the only way to get back my baby boy. Within two weeks of the phone call, my baby boy was back in my arms. I had enrolled Nicole into a private all-girl Christian school and Logan into kindergarten. With the help of my now new neighbor, transport to school was easy as his daughter the same age as Nicole was going to the same school. He even helped with Logan, picking him up from school as he worked the night shift.

Having John and Mary next door was a saving grace. We became best of friends. Mary gravitated toward Logan. She longed to have a son but was unable to have any more children. Little did I know that she and John had just reconciled their marriage after a five-month separation. Having Randy and I as friends, we did a lot together. We encouraged them daily, and soon, their love began to blossom again. How ironic. A broken couple to help another fix their marriage. Just the hand of God at work, I guess. We went to church together when we could. There was a new meaning to life again. Hope did not seem dead after all. Randy found a job at a travel agency, and life was back to normal again.

It was that time for my mom to make her once-in-three-years visit to South Africa again. This time, things were so different from the last time she had seen me. Everything was set in place, and we seemed happy again. Or things only appeared to be. Any little love I may have had for Randy, by this time, was overshadowed by pure resentment. *How could I have come this far and still be breathing?* I wondered. My mom arrived, and the discussions of settling overseas began again. Once again, unbeknownst to me, God was aligning things to make preparations for my move to the US. Randy's job with the travel agency was the ideal thing. Pretty soon, our passports and visas were applied for. Within weeks, we received them with approved visas to travel to the US. I knew God was intervening as the visa process could be tedious and difficult to be approved, but here we were, no second interview, and all approved. Yes, I had to pull some strings to get some financial documentation submitted, but it all worked out for good. There was no more gambling or drinking or infidelity—for now.

Randy was given the opportunity to pay for our tickets during the course of the year. By December, he completed paying for three tickets—Nicole, Logan, and myself. The plan, all along, was that I go with the kids first, and Randy was to join us after a few months. Excitement grew as time drew closer to December 15, 2000. I was going to finally be on my way. I sold most of my furniture to rack up extra cash for my travels. Everything was going as planned. Randy was staying back to come and join us at a later date as we agreed. Finally, December 15, dawned. Excitement filled the air, for me at least.

As I walked into the kid's bedroom for the last time, I saw Logan's face was swollen. I immediately recognized the enemy's plan to disrupt this journey and the plans that God had in store for me. Immediately, I placed my hands on his face and began to pray and plead the blood of JESUS over my son. Nothing was going to stop me today! Randy, realizing that that this trip was now a reality, begged me to stay until the new year, and for the first time, I felt in control and stood my ground. I was boarding Swiss Airlines that night! We gathered our luggage, said our goodbyes to neighbors and friends. Mary was distraught and never liked goodbyes. She hurriedly hugged me and the kids and ushered out quickly before she could cry. With a heavy heart, we departed for the airport.

Still in prayer mode silently, I turned around to take one last look at Randy and all that I was leaving behind. For the first time, I saw Randy emotional. Call me cold or without emotion, I was not moved by his emotional state. The biggest secret during the time of planning this trip, I knew that I was never coming back to South Africa no matter what. I got my chance at freedom at last. Yes, I was still married according to South African law but, at least, some peace and joy at last—for now at least.

As the plane taxied down the runway, I stayed in prayer mode, thanking God for all that He had done and all for that lay ahead. I was going into uncharted territory. As the 747 jet took off, I broke down, sobbing and praying. That night, I left everything, including memories, experiences—good and bad—on that runway. My past suddenly seemed to fade into the distance.

CHAPTER

8

The fourteen-hour flight to Switzerland seemed never ending, but the adrenaline kept me awake. Logan and Nicole took several naps during the flight. Early hours of the morning, as we descended into Zurich airport, the snowed-capped mountains caught my attention. What a beautiful sight! I had never seen anything like this. This was my first time travelling abroad. My luggage was checked in directly to Miami, so I did not have to deal with that on my connecting flight. As we disembarked this flight, I immediately headed for the next boarding gate. There was a two-hour layover, but I was not taking any chances of missing my connecting flight. We were able to get some breakfast and refresh ourselves. And then to my surprise, the swelling on Logan's face had all disappeared as though it was not even there in the first place. He was back to being himself. The enemy was defeated—again.

Soon, it was time to board our connecting flight to Miami. It was another twelve hours of flying. Here we were, on our second leg of our journey. During this time, I got to think about the possibilities that awaited me. Firstly, I had not seen my sister, my nieces, and nephew since they left in 1995. *What does the future hold for me?* I thought. Fear of embracing a new lifestyle made me a little nervous, but God reminded me that He was in control. If He brought me this far, He was not going to leave me now. "For your word is a lamp unto my feet and a light to my path" (Psalm 199:105). God had delivered me from the hands of violent men and from those who have purposed to make my steps stumble (Psalm139:4). I felt, for the first time, a burden lift from my shoulders. I felt excitement and peace which I could not understand.

As the hours ticked by and followed our journey on the flight tracker screen in front of me, I dozed off into a deep sleep. I had no idea how long I was asleep. By this time, we were already flying over New York. A few more hours, and my new life adventure would really begin! I could not believe all of this was happening. For a moment, I felt like I was in a dream, but looking out the window, I realized this was no dream. I was actually going to be in the land of my dreams at last.

Preparing to land in Miami airport, I was asked to complete our I-94 cards. Hurriedly, I completed them and handed them over to the flight attendant who was so sweet. As we disembarked the plane and walked down the corridor, the first comment that Logan made was, "Why is this place so grey? It's so boring!" Laughing at his comments, we hurried toward the immigration line. I handed our passports to the officer who, at first, did not look friendly at all.

"What is the purpose of your visit? How long will you be staying? Are these your children?"

My response was calm and collected, "We are here to visit my ailing mom, who will be meeting her two grandchildren for the first time. We will be here for three months as our visas had allowed us to stay." But all the while, I was a nervous wreck but maintaining the friendliest smile ever, at the same time, trying to be as charming as possible because the truth was, my mom was not ailing, she had just seen her two grandchildren eight months ago when all the planning for this trip started, and last of all, I had no plans to return to South Africa. Something I could never ever divulge to anyone, least of all the immigration officer seated across from me. By this time, with my charm, I had managed to get a smile from the officer on the other side of the glass. (I had no doubt that God had already worked all of this out.) Within two minutes, we were all done, stamped, and approved to enter the United States of America.

I turned around, picked up Logan, grabbed Nicole by the hand, and without turning to look back, darted for the luggage carousel. To my surprise, our luggage was one of the first ones to appear. Grabbing the first cart nearby, I grabbed our luggage one by one off the carousel. Mind you, these bags were not lightweight at all. With the thought that I was never returning to South Africa, I brought as much as I could. Dumping them onto the cart, Logan hanging off my hip, and Nicole holding onto my jacket, we darted off toward the arrival gates. The doors opened, and the sounds of my nieces' excited screams filled the air! They had managed to sneak under the security rope. Within moments, we were embraced in a hug, leaving us almost out of breath. My sister could hardly contain her excitement as we had been apart for five years. Hurriedly, we headed for the exit, and there, approaching in a burgundy Cadillac, was my mom.

Tears of joy rolled down our faces as we hugged each other. Our years of being separated had finally come to end. My mom left South Africa when I was the tender age of thirteen. Becoming a widow at the young age of thirty-two years, my mom struggled to cope with three young children in an old-fashioned culture and community. My mom was not a traditional Indian woman but one of a modern era, way ahead of her time. Feeling trapped by culture and society, she chose to seek a way of adventure but also to prepare a way for us for the future. So here I was, after many years of sacrifice and hard work, her dream of having me with her again finally dawned.

As we travelled through the famous I-95 interstate, I was totally amazed how different everything looked. Almost just as I imagined and saw on television and in the movies (*Miami Vice*). First stop was to meet my stepdad for the first time in person. (We had spoken over the phone over the years.) Mr. James Madison, the person who had made all my mom's dreams come true, who loved and cared for her ever so dearly. What a pleasure! And above all a Christian. Evening was dawning, and we had to leave so we could get settled in. The time zone change and jet lag was creeping in. We arrived at my sister's two-bedroom apartment where we would live for the next two years. (At first, all sharing the space, and later, just us.)

And so life began, December 16, 2000. One thing did not change, and that was Randy's control over my life. He may have been 7,830 miles away, yet he still controlled my life by the fear that I had for him, and he very well knew that was his triumph card. I had to call him every day, at least two times per day. I was not allowed to go anywhere without seeking his permission, and in most cases, I would rather just stay at the apartment rather than to go through the third degree of questions and still end up not being able to go. My fear was facing him and then having to go through accusations and threats for the times we were apart. Randy was the extremely jealous and possessive type. How I did not see anything wrong with that for so many years, only God knows the answer to that. Randy's mind was now out of control as now he had no physical control over me, and the fear of me ditching him became more real although I did not think of our marriage in that way. So the only way to try to control me was keep me in fear of my life with threats. As the days passed, the conversations were only quarrels with only demeaning comments from him about me and my family and for no apparent reason. Over the years, that's how Randy managed to destroy every confidence I may have had and kept me in low self-esteem. As December passed into January 2001, things only got worse between us. The only thing that kept me was my Jesu, consoling me each day with his precious and powerful word.

Time for Randy's departure from South Africa was drawing close. The plan was for him to turn in the keys for our apartment, collect the deposit, and head for Miami with the ticket he was supposedly paying for through the year. Came to find out, he had gambled his entire salary, including the deposit for the apartment, lost the balance of his ticket money, or so he claimed, and he had to move in with some friends because he had no place to stay since he terminated the lease earlier than he should. Once again, I was in the middle of his mess, and according to him, it's my responsibility to fix it. By this time, I had managed to clinch a job opportunity with one of my sister's friends who owned a mortgage company. Nicole and Logan were enrolled into the school system, and that enabled me to go to work. But the phone calls never stopped, and the quarrels got worse. January 27, 2001 Randy finally arrived in the United States. By borrowing six hundred dollars from my sister's then boyfriend, we managed to buy Randy's ticket to come over. Why? I just don't know!

The first few months, all was well as everything was new to him, and my mom, now retired, was able to spend time with us, taking us around, and trying to teach us the ropes. No more quarrels or jealous outbursts, no gambling or drinking, which was good. Days turned into months, and Randy could not find any work. Neither one of us had authorization to work in the US, and getting cash-paying jobs "under the table" was the only option. Working in a store was the last thing that Randy ever imagined himself doing. For the first few weeks, it seemed fine. Then the late-night shifts became a problem for him plus catching the last bus home was even worse. So he decided give up on the job and stay home.

Months past, and aggravation set in. Now a new excuse to start quarrels. The blame game: "It is your fault we are here! It's your family's fault for misleading us! I should have never left South Africa!" This went on for months. The positive thing was that he did not take to alcohol, and the urge to gamble seemed to be submerged, for now anyway. One fateful day, he was invited to go to the local horse racetrack. The beginning to an end I would call it. So another wave rolled in. I was now working to feed our family, pay bills, and feed his gambling habit which started to take a regular pattern again. By this time, my sister moved away to Fort Lauderdale with her children so she could be closer to the university as she was completing her degree in teaching. So here we were, struggling to survive.

My mom ensured we had all the necessities in our home. We had now started on our applications for immigration to remain in this country. My mom, being a US citizen, was our sponsor. With that in place, it was a matter of time before we would have authorization to work here. As fate would have it, immigration screwed up our applications, and that threw our case into a backlog. So it meant we still work under the table. This was not an easy time for us at all. By this time, we had found a church which we regularly attended. Prayer and the word of God were my solace.

Meanwhile, time was running out for me on my job. My boss saw an opportunity to take advantage of my situation. Sexual harassment! By the grace and power of the Lord, I was able to take a stand against this behavior, and obviously, he was afraid of the threats I made to report him to my mom and my sister since he was supposed to be a family friend. By December of 2001, he relieved me from my job because there was no way I was going to give in to this sexual harassment.

I got home that afternoon, got on my knees, and cried out to God. I trusted that God was going to have me in another job by the end of that week. I had already made a lot of contacts and had taught myself how to process mortgages. A few phone calls, and by the end of that week, I had an interview for another job at a mortgage company. With all confidence in the Lord, I walked into this interview. The manager was very impressed. All I had was a valid US driver's license which I produced, and I thought, *Here goes nothing.* The manager disappeared down the hall with my license. A few minutes later, she emerged with a big smile on her face and said, "The job is yours, when can you start?" A God-sent miracle this was! Overjoyed, as my mom and I rode back home, we prayed with thanksgiving. "Oh, come and taste of the lord and see how good he is." For sure.

A month passed, and I was so happy, the kids were happy, our household was peaceful. God was so good that I was able to hook Randy up with yet another job as an account receivable/payable clerk with a well-renowned shipping company. The pay was excellent, and we managed to get a "temporary social security number" for him to work. All was well again. And then the biggest surprise of all times—I fell pregnant. *How could this happen now,* I thought—new job, new in this country, and an unstable husband. At the age of thirty-five, and I was so afraid to tell my family that I was having yet another baby. Abortion was not an option. My faith would not allow me to do such a thing. Besides, I had to trust that my Lord would help me through all of this. I had already been through so much worse.

Somehow, putting aside all fear, I told my sister first and then had her tell my mom and brother when he showed up in April to surprise my mom for her birthday. Giving Randy the benefit of the doubt, my family accepted this. The next few months was peaceful but trying as I experienced some complications in my pregnancy. Being age thirty-five, I stood a few risks, Down syndrome being one of them. Various tests were done, and since we had no history of birth defects in our family, the tests were good. Fasting and prayer was a priority. That gave me the assurance that all will end well, and I was going to have a healthy baby.

As the months closed in, I was almost fully prepared to welcome another baby after seven years. Logan was in second grade, and Nicole was in high school now. A great challenge awaited me. The support of my mom, stepdad, and my dear sister was astounding.

A few weeks before I could finish off for my maternity leave, I discovered condoms in the glove compartment of our car. These can only belong to one person, and so I asked. And the result, a lie and then a lame excuse. That night, I went through Randy's wallet and found the answer—phone number to one of his floozies. Whether she knew he was married or had kids, I had no clue. So the next day, I called the number only to find out yes, she knew him and had been fooling around with him, but he had denied that he was married or had any kids, let alone another one on its way. I confronted Randy that evening, and obviously, he denied everything which he was so good at, and he allowed his friend to take the fall for him. I refused to believe anything, and eventually, it led to a heated quarrel which ended up in Randy putting his hands on me yet again. Nine months pregnant, and here we are again. But this time, he controlled himself because, now, my mom was within reach, and the law was not to be played with here. A few weeks later, it was time to bring another baby into this world, my world—what was I thinking?

A beautiful baby boy was born. For the first time, Randy was present in the delivery room to witness the birth of our son. This was the most beautiful experience any mother could have. It was like what you see on these hospital television series, only this time, I was in it. Nothing else mattered now. Just staring at my beautiful baby boy. This time, he was very light skinned, with the pinkest lips, and the most beautiful eyes, almost to cause Randy's family from South

Africa to make a comment that he may not be Randy's son. They said he looked Chinese (chuckle).

My family and my new friends all awaited eagerly to see me and the new arrival. My mom had just been three weeks out of surgery. She had a cancerous tumor removed, but nothing was going to stop her from seeing her new grandson. She had missed out on the growing up of all the other grandkids. She certainly was not going to miss anything again. Little Josiah was going to give her all the fulfillment she needed as a proud grandma. *Josiah*, a name given to me by the Lord. I had a sense that he was going to grow up and maybe, someday, be a faithful man of God.

A month later, Josiah was dedicated to the Lord at our local church. It was a beautiful celebration, having the entire family present. Within three months, I had to go back to work. Here again, God showed up. My mom was not in a condition to take care of little Josh, but my neighbor offered to babysit. Only the work of the Lord because I was fearful of putting him so young into daycare, especially with all the news of neglect and abuse we were seeing on the local news. Mom visited Norma every day and spent her time with Josh.

Time passed. I had moved on to another mortgage company to help a friend start his business. Randy was progressing at the shipping company too. Suddenly, life seemed to take a turn for the best this time.

CHAPTER 9

The apartment was now a little tight with three children. So we found a new three- bedroom apartment closer to my job, and now that Josh was close to almost completing two years, I figured I could put him in daycare. On qualifying for the apartment, it was under my sister's name as we were still not in a position to work legally yet. We moved into our new apartment and started a new adventure. Each episode in our lives was always starting something new. Nicole was now completing her last year of high school, Logan was headed to middle school, so all seemed to be in place.

Until one day, I found Randy in a panic one evening after getting home from work. He had taken money from the petty cash box at work without permission, and it was discovered before he could replace it. How long he was doing this, I had no idea. This meant that he had started gambling again. And this meant trouble yet again. This matter now escalated so fast that Randy was in danger of being prosecuted. My poor mom raced to his work and pleaded with management not to proceed with legal proceedings. She was apologizing for something she had no fault with. If I knew my mom, I think she paid the debt, and all went quiet after that. However, the embarrassment was on me as I had arranged that job for Randy. Fortunately for me, by that time, I had confided in my friend about the gambling problem and the financial issues I was having as I had to borrow money the one time from him to pay our rent. He knew me well and had seen my true personality. Here I was, at the mercy of someone else trying to get out of a mess that was not mine—again. We were on that stretch of parched road once more—Randy forcing money out of me, putting the children and the bills as no priority. His excuse, he was trying out his chances to make us more money.

Once again, I was able to hook him up with another job, this time at a mortgage company. Pay was excellent. Back on the gravy train, and all things well. Life started to look good, and prosperity abound. Randy had stopped drinking alcohol completely. Gambling seemed to be of no interest now. Nicole was graduating with honors from high school. Randy was so proud he decided to give her the biggest graduation party. We had booked the clubhouse and threw the grandest party for our baby girl, her dad's princess. That was an awesome year. As the year lease 2005 was closing in, we were financially stable and decided to move to a more secure community. I had found the perfect townhome for us—secure and affordable. In 2006, we were the tenants of a brand-new townhome. With this home, we had the opportunity to buy some furniture items the owner was selling as he sadly was going through a divorce, resulting in him having to lease this place as he still owned an apartment as well.

Yet another chapter started in our lives, not knowing how our lives were about to change. The events that was going to unfold in the next year would change our lives forever. For now, life was a bliss. If only life was this simple and pure, how happy we could be in our marriage and our home. It was times like these that always kept me hoping over the years that, someday, Randy would change and be the husband and father that I so longed for. Both Randy and I were working, kids at school, Nicole signed up for college, and she had a part-time job her grandpa organized for her. And then, one day, just like a tornado without any warning, our household was turned upside down. I could not understand any of this. Here I was, faithfully trying to serve the Lord, attending church regularly, and then all this turmoil.

Randy started gambling in the races again. His paycheck going in all to the races. I was struggling with the bills once again. Making sure the kids had just what they needed came with huge sacrifices. I questioned the Lord over and over again. I was getting torn apart being the pawn in a game I knew I could never win. Daily sacrifices had to be made just so we could continue. Randy had become so paranoid by this stage that even the kids and I could not have any conversations without him accusing us of plotting schemes against him. I was separated from my family. I started to withdraw. Low self-esteem, lack of confidence was the order of my days.

My mom was the only one visiting almost every day, yet Randy was always pleasant in her presence. One thing for sure, he respected my mom despite all his shortcomings; in fact, they got on very well. My mom always tried her best to show him love although she knew I was suffering a great deal. She never pried into our marriage no matter how much she wanted to, but I was her daughter. What mother could stand by and see her child suffer. My mom just went from day to day, ensuring we had the necessities. My day started with prayer, trying to seek refuge in the Lord, looking for guidance, trying to do right by the Living Word. My Bible was my only source of comfort and my place of refuge was at the feet of JESUS. I envied the other couples at church. *Why could I not have that, Lord?* But the Lord was working behind the scenes, and I just did not know it.

Celebrating my mom's sixty-seventh birthday was one of the hardest things for me to do. How do I celebrate when my life was in turmoil? None of my family members had a clue of the things that were transpiring behind closed doors. In any event, we celebrated this occasion in honor of my beautiful mom. Things started to spiral downwards and fast too. The worst thing that a mother can do is ask her children to tell a lie. What was I teaching my kids? I had to ask forgiveness, but how else was I to keep the peace in the presence of the children? I kept the quarrels between Randy and I behind closed doors as much as I could. I tried to keep them away from witnessing the beatings, hiding my bruises by covering up. They were now at an age where they could understand. How could I protect them from this? How much longer could I keep them away from this? All these questions with no answers. I felt so alone. Thoughts of suicide surfaced again. But this time, I had little Josiah to think about too. Then it happened!

Pressure was starting to build, and Randy's anger were now being directed toward the children. A few months before, he suspected Nicole may have acquired a boyfriend. The fact he discovered that he may be of black descent infuriated him. Randy had grown up during the era of apartheid, the same as me. The difference was, my parents did not teach us to discriminate between color, but Randy was taught differently I guess—old fashioned, with color discrimination. So in reality, his only daughter, the apple of his eye, dating someone of color was not acceptable. He confronted her one evening, and being so afraid of her dad, she disputed everything she was asked. Here I was, standing right in front, unable to defend my only daughter as, firstly, this was news to me, and second of all, I stood no chance of defending her because, at that moment, Randy accused me of knowing all along and that I lied on her behalf to cover up for her. There was no reasoning with him when he was in this state. He demanded she produce her cell phone, but she refused to comply, and without warning, he slapped her right across her face so hard that I felt the pain rip through my body. I stood frozen for a moment. How could I not protect my child against this monstrosity? Intervening just made things worse. But I lunged forward to try and protect her from him lashing out again. We spent hours in terror while he interrogated us with questions. All I could do was pray under my breath, asking God to intervene. Such terror caused by your own parent who claimed to love you, promised to protect you from harm, yet here he was doing the very thing he promised to protect you from. The kids could never comprehend this—ever. It just did not make sense.

Nicole withdrew completely, spending most of her time out of the house, trying to occupy her time with her college classes and focusing on keeping up her grades. To a great wonder, both children were A-grade students throughout their years in school. Praise the lord for his blessings on them. Nicole drifted away from us. One thing that I never realized, there was no time for shared love between me and the children. I was too preoccupied with how we were going to survive the next day. I was completely oblivious of the children's feelings or what they must have been through all this time. Does that make me a bad parent?

A few weeks later Randy cornered Logan who was only twelve at this time and was demanding to know how his cell phone bill was paid. Logan, confused and scared trying to cover up for me, was caught in a lie. The poor kid had no knowledge of how to handle this. He was afraid of his father. We all were! Before I could intercept, Randy had landed a slap right across Logan's face. The child was in a state of shock; this was the first time something like this had transpired. My thoughts were, *What is going to happen when Logan gets into his teenage years? Was he going to fight him like a man, or would this be the way he would behave with his brother when they got upset with each other?* I saw them action many times, and there was nothing pleasant with it. And then it hit me! I had to do something about this life. I cannot sit back and allow my kids to be abused and mistreated. Besides, the fear he instilled in us was overwhelming, yet he truly believed that we had no reason to be afraid of him. *How* I may have taken abuse for many years, but now my own children, and I can't protect them? Something had to be done! Something had to be done NOW!

CHAPTER 10

Our household remained cold and silent for months. By this time, I started working from home. The pay was not great, but it helped to get us through.

One afternoon, Randy stormed in from work during his lunch hour. He came in demanding money from me, and I knew the reason all too well. I didn't have any, and the quarreling started. A few minutes later, Nicole walked in. I knew instantly he was going to pick a fight with her too. All too soon! The next thing I remember, he had us both in the living room, interrogating us, and the topic went to the suspicions he had all along about a certain person of color that Nicole was dating. Just then my cell phone rang, Randy grabbed it and threw it to the floor. As it hit the floor, it shattered into pieces. Before I knew, Randy reappeared with a baseball bat in hand. My body was trembling with fear but, moreover, that Nicole was in the same room, and there was no telling what he would do next. He yelled and demanded answers to the interrogating questions. Now it didn't matter whether I responded or not; to him, everything was a lie, and everybody was lying to him. When he was in these moods, even if he was told the truth, it just did not matter. Before I could blink an eye, I saw him raise the bat toward Nicole. Probably trying to scare her into telling the truth, but I was not taking any chances. I lunged forward and grabbed the bat. That sent him into a further rage. He swung the bat in my direction, and by the grace of God, I managed to block with my hand. It certainly had to be a supernatural moment because, although it grazed my arm, I did not feel the full impact. Nicole sat there horrified. The next minute, Randy just turned and stormed out of the house.

I tried to console Nicole who was, by this time, hysterical. I tried to console her, but that was not solving our problem. How could I allow this to continue? My mind was racing; my body trembled with fear. What was I going to do? Logan had become completely withdrawn. Our home was no longer a home but a house filled with terror, not knowing when the next storm would rage.

I remember trying to consult with our church counselor, and all I got was you have to leave him, but how? No immigration status! Where do I go? I reached out to one of my friends who I considered close, but I got the same response. Prayer was the only thing I could hold on to as though my life depended on it. Days passed, and all I could think of was how was I going to get out of this. This was never going to stop. I prayed something would happen to Randy while he was out, wishing something bad could happen so I will have a way out. That was not the right thing to do, but I was trapped. And so were my children. I eventually started a new job as a consultant, and things were quiet for a while. Sunday church days were my consolation and time of real peace. Coming home, thereafter, and pretending everything was okay was one the hardest thing to do. Just keeping the peace for the sake of the kids. And the fateful day happened!

I heard the phone message on the answering machine that Randy was locked up at the local police station! I had to think and think fast! But was I really thinking? Should I go down to the police station? But which one; he didn't say! Call me selfish, the thoughts after that was all about me! I knew staying to rescue Randy would only allow the reign of terror to continue. Besides, he would have found some way to hold me responsible for this situation (even though I was far from blame) as he had become paranoid about almost everything. And then, like lightning, my first thought was to RUN!!

As we drove around the shopping mall area, fear gripped me. Where am I to go where Randy will not be able to find us. I did not want my family involved as there was no telling what Randy would do. Besides, they did not know much about my life of terror except for the odd gambling issue when I had to borrow money from them to pay bills. By this time, evening had already set in. Nicole was crying hysterically, Logan with a confused look, and little Josh had no clue what was going on. My only saving grace now would be to call my mom and stepdad. Within a few minutes, my stepdad and mom pulled up behind the shopping mall where we were hiding. Between tears and hysteria, I tried explaining to them what had just happened. Going to my mom's house was not a choice as I knew that would be the first place Randy would look for me. Whether those threats he had made over the years and again just a few weeks ago would be carried out, I was not sticking around to find out! My mom was furious as it seemed like there was absolutely nothing she could do to help us. My stepdad insisted I take the money he was giving to me to ensure we had enough to stay at a hotel.

After driving around for an hour, not knowing what the next step is, we eventually booked into a local inn for the night. Once in the room, I broke down. The reality of the situation hit me. My mind had snapped. Maybe even a type of nervous breakdown. Nicole managed to calm down Logan and Josh and settle them into bed. There was no turning back now. But where do we go from here? That night, I did not get much sleep. Waking up the next morning made me realize that was not just a nightmare but reality. I actually had managed to get away from Randy for the first time in twenty years.

My only option this morning was to call the crisis line. I did not want my family involved. I did not want Randy to think that they had any part of this. This was not planned but a truly spontaneous decision on my part. I was given several locations where we could be safe. All the locations were several hours away from Miami. Sitting alone in the hotel room, I had to formulate a plan of action. After several calls, now all I had to do was await a response. Hours seemed like days on end.

As afternoon closed in, a phone call from the landlord brought me back to reality. The police had shown up at the house as the neighbor thought someone was trying to break in, not realizing that

Randy was released from jail, and he was trying to get into the house. This was the first time I thought about what Randy was going to do. He had no clue that I had run off with the children. After a discussion with the police and the landlord over the phone, I explained my situation and confirmed that Randy was my husband. I told the landlord to let him in only to take a few of his belongings. Under police guard, Randy, totally confused, was allowed into the house to retrieve some of his belongings. It was only then Randy realized what the real situation was. He apparently called up a friend to pick him up where he stayed the night. Not until this very moment did I think about Randy's situation. Here I was, running away for my life, and yet, I had compassion for Randy. He had no family here, and there was no way my family was going to put him up.

I begged God forgiveness. I had no intention of hurting or getting back at Randy. I just wanted us to be safe. I knew Randy would now start the search for us. First stop, my mom's house. My mom told Randy she knew nothing of this and asked for an explanation. Not sure of what he told her, he headed off quickly to avoid further questions. The next day, I got confirmation that we had a location of refuge. Now was the time to make my move. Up to this day, I cannot explain my state of mind during all that was transpiring.

In haste, I made a decision to clear the house out. I arranged a U-Haul 26-foot truck and headed home. I had to trust in the Lord fully that Randy was not going to show up while we were at the house. I stopped at the guard gate and advised the guard on duty not to allow Randy through if she saw him and to call the police if she did see him. With two of Nicole's school buddies, we started to clear the house and pack up the truck. I was calm and collected as we rounded the last few items. Suddenly, Nicole ran into the house screaming hysterically! Randy was at the gate! My body tensed, and I was immediately overwhelmed by fear. Trying to stay hidden, I dialed 911 for the first time. I was not taking any chances this time. Within minutes, the police arrived, just in time to calm down the situation at the gate as well. Randy was furious for not being able to enter. As the police sergeant approached the house, feverishly, I tried to explain my situation. The sergeant was horrified at the things he heard, and he documented everything. Now I had a recorded case against Randy. He tried to calm me down by reassuring me that he will not let any harm come to us. Randy had requested from the police officer that I give him his passport and the rest of his belongings. Hurriedly, I threw his belongings into garbage bags and handed his passport to the officer but keeping out of Randy's sight. I requested the sergeant and the officer to wait a few more minutes for us to finish packing and to escort us in case Randy showed up again. I dropped off the keys at the real estate office with instructions of how the landlord could reach me so we could bring this chapter to a close.

Within hours, we were finally on the road. A lonely, scared woman with three young children heading to an unknown destination just to be safe. Driving a 26-foot truck with a full load I had never done before. But here I was! Looking at Nicole, I saw her breathe a sigh of relief. Logan also seemed relieved for the first time. Now little Josh was just all curious. We told him that we were going on an adventure. He loved adventures. And so did our journey begin.

CHAPTER 11

Several hours had passed, and we stopped to grab a bite to eat. As we travelled further and further away from Miami, more relief set the mood. The children seemed happy, and that made me feel happy. As we journeyed for the next five hours, it seemed our destination was close. Roads all unfamiliar to me, we managed to find the location. There was nobody on the location, so another hour was spent waiting for someone to show up, only be told that there was no place at this location for us. My heart sank immediately as I buried my face into my hands and broke down. *What have I done?* Taking my kids to an unknown place only to be confronted with something worse. I had never seen Nicole take on the responsibility of an adult as she tried to console me. Even Logan was trying to reassure me that everything was going to be okay. As evening was drawing close, we decided to get a room for the night. We needed the rest anyway.

The next morning, I called a friend to see if she could help us find accommodation. Meanwhile, God was at work again. It seemed He knew all along where we would spend the next few weeks. Her mom lived alone in this enormous house, and she was willing to take us in. What a blessing! She lived only thirty minutes away from where we were. So we decided to put all the furniture into storage. I remember, in the intense heat, Nicole, Logan, and myself unloaded this 26-footer truck. My heart broke as I looked at my two children working their hearts off just so we could have peace and be safe. After several hours of unloading, we called a cab and headed to our new destination.

As the cab pulled into this long circular driveway, I became nervous as this was all new to us. No one was home, but we were advised earlier where we would find a key to get into the house. As we settled down for the night, we all seemed to be more relaxed. We spent the next two days on our own as my friend's mother was away on a trip. The home was serene and beautiful. It was like living in a resort. Now I had to withdraw Logan from school with all that had been transpiring. I had spoken to the school principal, and he agreed to assist in any way he could. We had arranged for Logan to take his final tests as the school year was drawing to a close, and the following year, Logan would be going to high school.

The next day, I arranged for Nicole and Logan to travel back to Miami so he could take his tests. Hopping into a cab, they headed for the train station. This is how God was at work as even the cab driver, not knowing anything about our circumstances, seemed to find favor with the kids. He was concerned for their safety and insisted they call him on their return. I thank GOD for the money that my stepdad had given me as this was our source to get all these things done. The principal had taken the necessary precautions of safety while Logan took his tests. Nicole and Logan spent the night with a friend and boarded the train the following morning to head back. My family had no indication that the kids were in Miami. I had not been in contact with any of my family members since our departure on the fateful day. Putting my family through this stress was not fair and did not make sense, and the fewer people who knew, the safer we would be. The kids returned, and the summer vacation began.

A few days later, Mrs. Grayson, seventy-five years of age, humble woman of God but full of life, arrived home. We spent the rest of the evening getting to know one another. She was grateful for the company as she lived alone. She immediately took to little Josh. He was her Superman. She grew to love him rather quickly.

A few weeks passed, and I had to plan our next move. Something that never crossed my mind before, *How was I going to find a job with having no legal authorization to work in the Unites States?* I looked into a few opportunities, and unfortunately, they all required legal authorization for me to work. This meant that I would not be able to attain our own apartment either. A ROADBLOCK! Depression began to take its toll. I had to hold myself together. I was the adult, and I needed to take care of my children. They did not ask to be here, so it was my responsibility to take the reins.

As I arose one Tuesday morning, sitting at the breakfast table, my phone rang. It was my old boss. She was calling to check on me and the kids. Little did I know, God was about to blow my mind! "Seek ye first the kingdom of God and all righteousness and all these things will be added unto you" (Matthew 6:33). Her first response to me was they miss me, and that my job was still available, and they were willing to do all they could to assist me in my situation. My boss was fully aware of my situation as I had a discussion with her before I left Miami when I had to notify her that I would no longer be at work. Here we were, an opportunity, a job—something that we really needed to survive! And not just any job, but an old job with an assurance that we will also be safe (for a while anyway.) This was a no-brainer. My boss, being the compassionate person she was, searched for an apartment for us, secured one with her own money. It was all set. Within a few days, we got prepared to depart from our safe haven. Thanking Mrs. Grayson for her hospitality and her prayer and encouragement during our stay with her, we departed. Mrs. Grayson was sad to see us leave, but she knew we had to start somewhere again.

As we headed to the storage, we were excited at the proposition of the job but also nervous being on the same grounds as Randy again. It had been almost a month since we had any contact with him. Once again, in the extreme heat, Nicole, Logan, and I started to reloaded another 26-foot truck. Bearing in mind, Logan was only thirteen at this point, and here he was, doing this heavy labor meant for a man. God's grace was with us that day. We pulled out of the storage facility and headed toward the interstate. Within ten minutes of being on the road, I realized the braking system on this truck was faulty. With lights flashing, we headed to the closest U-Haul facility.

We were given a new truck, but now, it was the matter of unloading and reloading another 26-footer. We had just spent six hours doing just that. Without wanting to waste time, we started to unload and reload the new truck. Halfway through, two gentlemen approached and offered to assist us. They had been watching us while they were loading other trucks that day. Glory to God, we got finished sooner than anticipated. The kids and I were exhausted, but we were eager to get on the road. Another eight hours of driving, and we were closing in on our final destination. Halfway through, I called my mom and filled her in on our plans. She was ecstatic to hear that we were coming back. There was no talk about Randy this time.

As we approached the turn off to our destination, my mom was parked on the side of the road in her little blue car which we all knew so well. She ushered us on as we headed for the Comfort Inn just off the interstate. Here we were, in our new town, ready to start life again—just the four of us. As we pulled into the parking lot, the kids jumped out and ran to their grandma's open arms. Tears of joy overflowed as we all embraced. The office to the apartment building had already closed, so it meant spending one more night at a hotel. Bright and early the next morning, we headed down to the office of our new apartment building. My mom was already there. After filling out and signing the documents, we were ready to move in. For the first time, with the aid of my stepdad, I was able to get an apartment under my own name. It was a relief. It was a quaint two-bedroom two-bathroom apartment tucked away at the back of the community. Number 302 it was. I remember the expression on the kid's faces when they saw the apartment. Tears rolled down my face, just thinking what must have been going through their minds during all of this. We started to unload the truck for the last time. It was late evening by the time we were done.

Waking up the next morning was like in heaven. Pure bliss! I had the kids set up in the main bedroom as it would accommodate all three of them while I took the smaller of the bedrooms. Still very spacious and comfortable. I had left my car at my moms' house, so my stepdad had it fixed and ready for me. I was starting work the next day. As I drove to work that morning, I was very nervous. I knew that Randy had no clue about our whereabouts, but neither did I know where he was. There was no way he could follow me. He did not know where I was. Thinking I was just being silly, I parked my car at the back of the warehouse and headed in to work. What a welcome I received. I could not thank my boss for all that she had done. Apparently, Randy had been calling the office using a different name, every day. My boss was telling the truth; "I was not there," well, until this day (chuckle). Two days later, while I was in her office, the phone rang, and I got a glimpse of the caller ID. A familiar name of a mortgage company and knew immediately it was Randy. Once again, a different name and my boss's same response, but this time, she added that if these calls did not stop, she was going to call the police and report harassment.

Things started to look up for us. Nicole was back with her college classes and her job. Logan was enrolled in a new school, and Josiah was now ready for kindergarten. All of this was orchestrated by God. Logan was able to get to school by school transport, Nicole's college classes were across the street, and Josh's school was few blocks away. To be the icing on the cake as we could call it, I had taken on another position with my company, and the new office was just down the road. How much more could I ask for. God was at work, and I did not realize all of it. Life began to take on new meaning. I was in control of my life and had nobody telling me what needed to be done or, more importantly, nobody to take my money, no more gambling or dealing with drunkenness or fear, for that matter.

Two months passed by, and one evening, I got a call from a friend I used to work with a few years back. She seemed to get a little nervous as the conversation proceeded, and then she just blurted it out. "Randy was so sorry for everything that he had put me through!"

Astounded by her words, I asked what was all this about. She started to explain. While we were away, Randy had kept in contact with her. She found out that we had runoff without him. She mentioned that he would do anything if only he could be given another chance. At first, I was quite cold in my response. All the memories came flooding back. There was no way I was going to let him back into our lives. Besides, the kids, except for, Josh did not want to be near him. Relentlessly, she called every day and our conversation always ended up with Randy being the subject. But I still would not give in. Randy, by this time, had been put up in a Comfort Inn somewhere in Fort Lauderdale by his brother—the one person that I approached a year ago to ask for his help in regards to Randy's problem. He simply ushered me away and said it was a passing phase; he will be just fine. Well, Randy was now his problem. He was sending money from South Africa to help Randy survive. Randy did have a part-time job, but according to my friend, it was about to come to an end. His brother was prepared to buy him a ticket back to South Africa, but Randy refused, thinking he would get another chance to win back his family. So getting upset, his brother cut off funding his stay at the inn. In a few days, Randy was going to be put out on the street. Now why should I have cared? My compassionate nature, I guess. The memories of those dark days seemed so small. Not gone but just faded. With so little knowledge that the enemy was at work, this was the crack in the door which I let him in, not realizing the mayhem he had planned for us. If there was any time for me to have been sensitive to the Holy Spirit, that would have been the time. After much, much consideration, I decided to meet with Randy. Crazy and totally out of my mind! What was I thinking!!

Two days later, there I was standing at his door of the inn. I couldn't believe I was doing this. Mind you, this was being done without any knowledge to Nicole or Logan. I remember I made up some excuse to get Nicole to watch Josh for the day, and off I went. As the door opened, Randy fell to the ground, weeping like a baby at my feet. He couldn't believe that I was standing at the door that morning. Surprisingly enough, I did not feel an ounce of fear for him. He hugged me like there was no tomorrow. I remember spending the entire day with him just listening to apology after apology, then to find out why he was arrested. He was stopped for a nonworking taillight which led to a search of the car he was driving. In the car was found a small bag of marijuana. How that came to be, I had no idea. Randy was many things but, smoking marijuana, I didn't think so. He always had friends in his car, and Friday nights was always boy's night out, so that could have belonged to any one of his friends.

Somehow, Randy managed to get a misdemeanor. But now, he had a second record in the county, the first being the case of domestic violence that I reported on the day we were running away from him. But all of this didn't seem to matter now. Compassion overcame me, and the memories of the terror faded into the background. For him, this was his chance at making it all correct so he could win us back. In our conversation, he relayed his struggles during our absence. He went some days without eating because he did not have enough to pay for the room and buy food. He had to choose one. More compassion poured out this time. I opened the tiny fridge he had in his room, and it was empty except for half an orange. That happened to be part of his meal for the rest of the week. By this time, my heart was so heavy. I may have gone through hell with him, but no way could I see him suffer this way. He had made a friend at the inn next door where she allowed him to get breakfast in the mornings, but that was it. I walked him down to the local store to purchase a few food items for him. In all of this, not once did he ever ask where we had been or even where we were staying. He did not even ask or suggest to move in with us even though, in a few days, he was going to be without a place to live. Overcome with grief and compassion for him, I left him at his hotel room to head back home. I had so much to consider.

I got on my knees that evening and sought the Lord. I was torn between Randy and the kids again. I had to pluck up courage to tell the kids. Nicole flew into a rage, but I think it was more fear than rage. She would not have anything to do with this. We spent the entire evening arguing for the first time. I had never had a row with my kids before. Breaking down into tears, I realized, for the first time, that Nicole was not going to accept the decision I was about to make. Neither was Logan, but he did not comment. I remember the night I brought Randy to the apartment. The last time I saw that kind of fear in the kids was the day we had the confrontation at the house the day we were leaving. The kids felt compassion about their father not having food to eat but moving in with us was not the option they expected. Nicole left home and moved in with a friend.

It was the strangest feeling ever having Randy back in our lives. Logan was very distant to him. Randy tried to fit into our new schedule of life. He was helping out in the apartment more. He cooked and cleaned, even doing the laundry. Nicole refused to speak to me and just never came back home. Life continued, but I still stayed isolated from my sister and the rest of the family. My mom was the only one who came by regularly. She embraced Randy being there because her heart was bigger than mine. Months passed, and everything was calm and peaceful.

Josh grew closer to his father during this time. Also during this time, Randy acquired a job with a mortgage company out in West Palm Beach. Taking the commuter train everyday became a routine. Randy helped with the bills, and everything was going smooth. As far as my feelings for Randy, there was no love lost between us. I went from day to day. As long as there was peace in my home, that's all that mattered. I held the upper hand for the first time. Randy was well aware of his records with the county, so with that, we were able to maintain peace in my home.

Months passed, and Nicole came home one evening. Randy answered the door. He wept inconsolably and embraced her in a hug. After all, he loved the kids very dearly. With a little tension, we managed to get by the following months. My lease was up for renewal and the fact that Randy had moved in, the place was a little cramped. Besides, Nicole was now heading for twenty-two, and Logan was heading for fifteen. Sharing the room with Josh as well was a little tough. I had the option to upgrade to a three-bedroom, which we did do after a discussion. With three incomes, we would be able to manage comfortably.

12

Logan started high school, Nicole continued studying, and Josh was now grade two. My mom visited every day without fail. Picking up Josh from school became her daily chore. She insisted she wanted to do it, but it also gave us time together. By this time, I had started working remote as it was too expensive for the company to run an office. So my boss downsized but allowed me to continue working from home. A full office set up, I was able to perform my job comfortably.

Six months into moving into this new apartment, tension began to rise. I noticed Randy had started with the odd weekend horse racing again. I should have recognized the signs immediately. Not long, Randy was back into gambling again. No drinking at all but just addicted to horse racing. His excuse this time was making the big bucks so we could get our immigration paper completed. Weekends turned into week days. Dipping into his salary turned into gambling his entire paycheck. Pretty soon, items were being pawned to keep up with the bills but, more so, to feed his addiction.

Tensions, one day, flared, and we got into a big argument. Randy had gambled his entire paycheck that Friday, but he also knew I was due to collect my check too on that same day. With audacity, he accompanied me to my boss's house to pick up my check. When my boss saw him in the car, she knew exactly why he was there. The first time she saw him, she said nothing, but the expression on her face told it all. Then it started to be a habit. That was when the arguments started. At first, it was just back and forth arguing and him threatening me, but I guess, he was afraid to lay his hands on me for the fear of me calling the police on him. Although I was still very afraid of Randy and his temper, I never allowed the situation to escalate to a point that would cause him to start beating on me.

This day was like no other. He demanded I give him my entire check, trying to convince me that he will turn that into the million dollars he was always hoping to make for about thirty-some odd years. I remember standing in line at the cash-checking place, thinking how was I going to pay the upcoming rent and put food on the table. Moreover, I needed the utilities to stay connected because of my remote access for work. The most odd thing was, I always wondered if Randy ever considered the bills, the kids, their needs. There would be times when I asked him how we were going to manage to get these bills paid when he lost all the money at the races. Same responses that I had been hearing for over thirty years: "Don't worry, I will come back and pay it." Never happened. I was ALWAYS left to figure out the way to get things done. He felt no shame in having me go borrow money from wherever to sort the mess he made. I had no choice in the matter. Several occasions, I had to ask my sister to cover for me, and she always willingly did so especially for the sake of the kids.

There were still outstanding debts from the previous years which Randy owed but no responsibility whatsoever. There were debts that I paid to avoid being taken to court. There was this one case when a once known friend threatened to take Randy to court because he had an outstanding debt. I had to find my way to his office and plead with him not to proceed. To Randy, avoiding these people at all costs, he was good at, but putting me in the line of fire, he had no problem. But on this day, as he demanded my paycheck, he became more and more infuriated as I refused. While sitting in the car, he lashed out and grabbed me by the throat. Looking into his eyes, there was no emotion but just intense anger. To go back to the day I ever agreed to allowing him back into our home, I knew, someday, I would have to face the repercussions of my actions of running away and leaving him virtually homeless. This was now the season to face up. It's been a whole two years since that fateful day. Now it was time for payback. Off he went to the races that day, and I knew he wasn't coming back with any money.

I called my stepdad and asked for him to help me again as the rent was due. My stepdad tried to convince me to make a change, but I did not know how because I felt trapped by fear of Randy. In regards to our legal status to work, nothing had changed. I was still working under the table, so to speak. This was what I could never understand with Randy. Once the money was all lost at the track, he would come home and pretend like everything was okay. He would go out to the patio and smoke a pack of cigarettes at a time. Another habit I had to feed regularly. Given a choice between bread and cigarettes, cigarettes would trump that in most cases. Randy had worked several jobs over the years but could never keep any of them. He always ended up losing the best jobs because of his feverish habits.

Day in and day out, the same thing, same habits continued. Hiding money away became my way of life. Lying to Randy about not having extra money became a regular thing as time went on. I hated every moment of it. Trying to explain that this was not the way of life to Nicole and Logan was difficult as I had to lie in their presence and then having them to lie as well to Randy. What was I teaching my kids?? Keeping my purse out of sight all the time, making sure that Randy would not empty my wallet of what little I may have had in there, hiding my remaining pieces of jewelry was crazy. This was my own prison within a prison.

My poor mom would come by every day to ensure we had the supplies we needed. Emptying out her coins from her purse trying to help; I cannot imagine what must have been going through her mind. My mom was never confrontational about anything she saw in our home. She would make conversations just to keep her sanity, I think. Her mind must have raced through several things just sitting in our or home, after all, I was the baby of the family, and to see me struggle through life must have been heart wrenching for her. Leaving me behind in South Africa at such a young and tender age was one of the hardest things she had to do. She always carried a heavy burden through the years and tried her best to make up for lost time every time she could. During our several conversations we have had over the years, I always tried to reassure her that I never held any contempt for her for making such a courageous decision.

But here we were, together again after so many years of being apart, yet still so much turmoil surrounded us. Week after week, the same pattern ensued. Randy would come with me to collect my pay-check only to take it all away. My boss used to be livid at seeing him waiting in the car. It was my choice to make, but fear had me trapped. Soon, stuff from our home started missing. At first, Logan's video games started to go missing. Then his Playstation was gone. All of this without seeking his permission. I cannot imagine the thoughts that must have went through Logan's mind when he figured out that it was his dad who, at the time, lovingly bought him the best of games. It didn't matter how much they would cost, when he had the money, he bought it for Logan. The same applied to Nicole. She had the best clothes or the most expensive and fashionable brand-name sneakers.

I remember the one time when Air Jordans came into the market. He stood in the line at the store at five o'clock in the morning. All for his little princess. A few Christmas celebrations were fantastic. The strangest thing about Randy was, with all the quick-tempered problems he had, he had such a giving spirit, very compassionate side, and always willing to help those in need. If he had his last dollar in his pocket, and if someone really was in need, Randy would be the first to give it away. It was this behavior over the years that always kept me hoping that he would change someday. It was this hope that kept me being married to him for so long. It was the same hope that always blinded me to his abusive behavior toward me.

As the weeks turned into months, things only got worse. There were days when there was only bread and peanut butter to eat and milk for Josh. By that time, Nicole and Logan never questioned the situation. They both withdrew into a shell, and the saddest thing was that, I never noticed it. I was too busy trying to survive from one day to the next. Dealing with my emotions, trying to balance life between the children and Randy consumed every ounce of energy I had.

Then one weekend, as we were getting ready to attend a family event, I opened my jewel box to put on my wedding ring as I never left home without it. To my surprise, it was not there. Thinking I may have left it in the kitchen when washing up the dishes, I looked on the counter, still no sign. Frantically, I began searching. In twenty years, I had never mislaid my rings. The next thing to do was ask Randy if he had seen it, and he very calmly answered he had not. That entire evening, it bothered me trying to think where I could have left them. After searching for two days, and with Randy watching me search in those days, he finally admitted that he had pawned them to the local pawnshop. I was astounded. My mouth remained open, but no words were coming out. It should have been no surprise, but I truly never thought he would go that far. That was a symbol of our marriage, and the thought that he could do something like that only showed he did not value our marriage, and he had taken everything we had for granted. I was so angry that I could feel my ears burning up. For the next couple of days, I did not speak to Randy. He tried to reassure me that as soon as he got the money, he would retrieve my rings from the pawnshop.

For me. my engagement ring carried a symbol of our young love. On my twenty-first birthday, Randy proposed to me. On the evening of my grand party, which my brother and sister-in-law had planned, Randy showed up with this large shoebox. It was all wrapped up in the prettiest wrapping paper. Eagerly, I tore open the paper only to open the box to find a bunch of wrinkled newspaper filled inside. Thinking this was a prank, I discarded the box. Well, almost, if it was not for my brother who said take another look inside. As I rummaged through the newspapers, I found a little white box. Excited, I opened it—and it was empty. Now I was getting really upset. Randy stepped up and said to look again. There in the very corner of the box was small black velvet box. Thinking this, too, was a prank, I opened it. To my greatest surprise, inside lay the most beautiful eighteen-karat gold diamond ring—a diamond so visibly seen. I was lost for words. Everyone around me was clapping and laughing because they thought that was the coolest idea ever. Randy took the ring and placed it on my finger asking me to marry him. I looked at my brother, and he seemed pleased (at that time anyway), and I took it as his approval. During his speech at my party that night, he announced our engagement and wished Randy and I best wishes, but I also got the feeling it was also a warning sign for Randy to promise to take good care of me. Some promise that was!

So by Randy now pawning this ring—including my wedding band—after so many years of marriage, meant that he didn't really care for our marriage let alone me as his wife, who always faithfully stood by his side. Even as he promised to get my rings back, I knew it wasn't going to happen. As the months went by, Randy was laid off from his job as the real estate market was struggling to recover from the huge loss a few years back. Now that left only me with a job and the entire household to support, and above all, what were we going to do with Randy and his ugly habit of gambling.

I was seeking the Lord each and every day, praying for peace and protection, praying for God to open up new doors. There were days when the enemy's voice spoke loud inside my head, the voice that was keeping me trapped, but I did not know that at that time. Being enslaved by fear and not forgetting the abuse, I could not hear God's voice clearly. I did not realize the enemy had to keep me busy and distracted so that I could remain in my "Egypt." He would allow a glimmer of hope and come back with a vengeance and crush any hope that I had. The enemy used everything in his power to keep me from enjoying the full impact of God's *grace*. I was so deeply immersed in my troubles that even when I sought the Lord, my prayer requests must have been all wrong because there were times when I felt that God never heard me or answered any of my prayers. My prayers seemed like it only went as far as the ceiling of my apartment, no further. But I never gave up.

As February 2011, approached, I was laid off from my job, as now, I needed my immigration status to continue working. We had heard nothing from the state department for years now. Every time we called, it was the same answer; my case is pending. And little did I know that Randy was planning to return to South Africa for over a year, prior to him losing his last job. He had colluded some scheme with his brother. At first, it was to try to get his status changed before mine, which was ridiculous as my mom was our sponsor, and I would have had to get processed first. This I found out later when I opened a piece of mail from immigration as it was addressed to me. Confronting Randy about this would have been useless as he would have lied his way through this. Besides, the application was denied anyway. The important thing now was how do we survive, and what was the next step in our lives.

Now that I think of it, this was an amazing miracle of God. Here we were, both out of work, but from day to day, we had our needs met. This could only be the hand of God upon us. For me, the peace between Randy and I was the important thing. He was not thinking of the racetracks now but how to get out of this big black hole that was approaching us—and approaching at top speed. As we discussed the different ways and things we could do, our future still looked dark—in fact, very dark. We had reached the end of the road. Our dream of being in America was about to end, and badly too.

Randy had been talking to his brother in South Africa at this time, trying to figure out a way. That's when the idea of Randy returning to South Africa was initiated. Randy's brother had been a successful businessman and was in a suitable position to assist us in planning this move. He, too, had given his heart to the Lord. A seed sowed over the years, and God was watering it. For days, we discussed this plan, and it seemed like the logical thing to do.

I remember talking this over with my mom and, just the thought of me leaving, left a look of horror on my mom's face. I never once thought how this would affect my mom. She was at our apartment every day, trying to help us look for alternative ways in which we could stay here in the States. She brought us supplies and would empty her wallet of any money she had. This decision had affected my mom badly. By this time, my mom had already been showing signs of her not being well. Her health was deteriorating, and I did not notice as much as I should have because I was too caught up in my own issues.

By now, the kids had completely withdrawn and had no comment about the decisions we were making. Again, I did not pay attention, as I should have, to know what they were thinking or feeling about all of this. I got frantic calls from my sister daily trying to convince me that this was not a good idea. So did my brother, my aunt—all saying the same thing. But how were we to continue here? No status to work, and pretty soon, no way to renew our driver's licenses as we did not possess the most current immigration paperwork to do that. Above all, no retirement! What a mess!

Soon, the tensions began to rise just discussing all of this, which led to arguments. Randy felt we had wasted all these years in this country, when he could have remained in Africa and probably had been as rich as his brother! If he had stayed in South Africa, we could have been very well-off. If we had just stayed put in South Africa, we would not have been facing this situation now! If! If! If! All ifs, but that didn't help now.

I was collecting my last paycheck since I was let go from my job, and I thought this would buy us some much-needed time. I was so wrong to even think that Randy was thinking the same. Seeing cash made Randy go into another dimension. I could never figure out what kind of thoughts would go through his mind. I remember standing at the bedroom doorway, and Randy was insisting I give him the cash. He needed to go try his luck at the races one more time. Maybe this would be our meal ticket out of this mess. But I refused. The more I refused, the more infuriated he became. The angrier he became, the more fearful I got, but I stood my ground. Without warning, Randy lashed out. My ears rang out in pain. Before I could react, he grabbed me, shoved me into the bedroom, and shut the door behind him. Not thinking he was only an earshot away from the kids, he began his rampage. Before long, I was bleeding from a tiny cut on my head. My hair slide pierced my scalp when he struck. My body hurt so bad from the blows. The sound of his angry voice calling my name and threatening me rang in my head over and over again. I couldn't take anymore, and I nervously handed him the cash. He stormed out, and there was peace! Yes, for me, that was peace when he left

I remember going into the bathroom that day filled with anger and contention. The way I felt that afternoon had never felt so real. I felt as though someone had their hands around my throat and was squeezing what life I had left in me. I couldn't breathe. Gasping for air, I fell on my knees and cried to the Lord. "Lord, where are you? Do you see me?" And then the next few words I still remember so clearly, "Lord, if you don't do something today, someone is going to die in this apartment! I know it's not going to be me. My kids need me more! What are you going to do, Lord? I can't take anymore!" I wanted out more than I did the day I ran away. I screamed out—in silence!

The thing was, when Randy got into these angry moods, he would bring up things from the past, things that he thought I was doing wrong in his eyes—accusing me of having affairs, plotting against his life, wanting to get rid of him but, moreover, the time when I ran away with the kids and all that he had to endure during that time with no help from my family. That was the thing that supposedly hurt him the most. He did not realize that my family did not have any information about my plans, and I did not want them involved in my affairs. Despite all the turmoil I went through with Randy, my family did love him. Either pride or maybe ignorance kept Randy from admitting that he had a problem with gambling or the bad temper flares or getting the help he needed. He called it gossip if I told my family any of this. He was always paranoid about that. So in order to keep the peace, I kept my silence through the years. But now it was payback time for me.

Randy returned later that evening. As usual, penniless and somber. There was no conversation for the rest of the evening or the two days thereafter. I spent most of time in my bedroom seeking the Lord—seeking direction, wisdom, answers. All I wanted now was to get out, to breathe again. I could have sworn, on day two, as I was praying in my bedroom, that Jesus was standing in the corner of my room and tears were rolling down His face just looking at me. I felt my spirit lifted as I looked at what I thought was the image of my Lord. Still confused at what I thought I saw, I emerged from my bedroom. As I came out, the phone rang, and it was Randy's brother on the other end of the line. He had booked a flight for Randy to return to South Africa. In two days, he had to go to the airport where his ticket awaited him. The surprised look that appeared on my face at that moment was not that Randy had to leave but more that my Lord had heard me—this time, loud and clear as it would seem. Randy, on the other hand, seemed more confused and suddenly reluctant. Could this be really happening?

Randy called the kids together that evening, and for the first time in a long time, we had a family talk. He assured the kids that he was doing this for us as a family. He was going to go to South Africa and make us wealthy and be successful. This was all for us. I could tell that Randy doubted this decision about leaving here. Maybe he thought that he may never see us again, or maybe I would choose to stay on and leave him in the lurch. I couldn't tell the thoughts he was thinking. All I knew, I agreed that he would go first and set up, and we were going to follow when the time was right. As far as the kids went, surprisingly, they felt sadness, but it was also going to be a time for peace, for a while anyway.

The next day, I pulled out the suitcases and started to pack for him. I packed all that I thought he would need. And that was almost everything he owned. My mom came later that day to say goodbye and that she was sad to see him go. To my surprise, Nicole gave her father three hundred dollars for his travel expenses. This, no doubt, showed she did love her father above all he had put us through. Logan did not show much emotion. I couldn't read him at all. As for Josh, he wasn't too aware of all that was transpiring. He thought his father was going on vacation. That night, none of us got much sleep. For one, we had to be at the airport by 4:00 a.m. The thoughts of what faced us from here on was going to be a challenge. Our ride to the airport on this day, March 17, 2011, was one of the quietest journeys ever. We lived ten minutes away from the airport, but the ride seemed to be the longest.

As we pulled up into the parking lot, emotions started to set in. Quietly, we all walked into the terminal, and Randy headed for the check-in counter. All done, and it was time to head for departure. As Randy was being checked in at the security, the TSA official seemed irate for some reason. I could see there was an issue with his passport, and Randy was trying to explain something to her, but she wouldn't listen. She called in for another official to inspect Randy's passport. I was suddenly overcome by fear because Randy did overstay his visa initially—we all did. Nervously, we stood watching and waiting as Randy tried to give the second official an explanation. Minutes later, Randy walked back, and I thought this was all over. Oh my god! As Randy approached me, I tried to ask Randy what was going on, and his response was so angry and disrespectful to me that it quickly reminded me why he should board that plane. I was trying to help, and he shut me down. That could not have happened at a better time as I was about to tell Randy not to go, not to leave. Yes, sounds crazy, I know, but that was the exact thing that almost came out of my mouth. The reminder came at the right time. I retreated and remained quiet.

Randy gathered us around to pray, asking God to protect us while he was away and that God may give us direction from here on. Yes, another strange characteristic of Randy; he did pray among all the turmoil he would put us through. Clearly all trapped in our EGYPT, I would call it. As Randy turned to embark on his journey, tears filled his eyes as he hugged and kissed the kids, telling them that he loved them so much. He turned to me, hugged me so tight, and said that he loved me always and forever. Struggling to let me go, he kissed me hard on the forehead and turned and walked away. As we all waved goodbye, we had no idea of what awaited us in the months to come. Randy disappeared down the aisle, and that was the last we saw of him.

With all of this transpiring, I should have seen this as a way of escape, but it was not. We were all feeling heartbroken. As dysfunctional a family we were, there was a strong bond between us all. As my sister drove us back home, there was no conversation in the car. My sister tried to reassure us that we were going to be okay; everything was going to work out. We got back to the apartment, and it was the strangest feeling ever. Peace, yes, but there seemed to be sadness in the air. The next day, Randy called to let us know that he had made it safely. He sounded excited to be with his brother, but there was a sadness in his voice. In the meantime, we tried to adjust to the new life. As I mentioned earlier, the deal was that Randy go to South Africa to set the foundation. He was to send money to us here while I sought to try to get another job. As the days passed, the peaceful atmosphere seemed to set in and the fact that Randy was no longer around. I had bought a five-dollar phone card which I used to call him daily. I kept the calls short so I could make many calls with it.

In the meantime. my mom continued to come by daily, sometimes, either taking Josh to school or picking him up afterwards. We spent days talking about everything that transpired and how the future may be. She wasn't thrilled at me wanting to leave the US. It was at this time I noticed her condition deteriorating. One day, she came in frantically. She had forgotten how to get to my apartment. She said she drove around for an hour trying to figure out how to get there. I became very concerned, especially now I had the time to focus on her rather than being caught up with my issues. I spoke to my sister about my mom's condition, and now that really caused much concern. We spent some days praying, and there were days when she seemed absolutely perfect. In the meantime, Randy had started working for his brother, and as usual, he made all these promises, like he did all the time, of all the great things he was going to do for us.

It was now the month of April 2011. We had begun to adjust to life, and for a moment, I thought this could all work out. There were still plenty discussions of us joining Randy in South Africa soon. Randy said that his brother was trying to arrange the tickets for us. He was going to send us the money to pay the bills while he put all the plans into action. I would have to get new passports for Logan and Josiah as Logan's had expired, and Josiah did not have one. Things were peaceful between Randy and me. We had proper conversations, discussing the plans for our future. Everything seemed the way it should, until Randy broke one of his first promises from our new plan. Time had come for the rent to be paid, and no money had been sent to us. Once again, I had to solve this mess. He was a million miles away, and here we go again with all this mess.

Frantically, I called my stepdad who came to my rescue once more. I had to make some decisions and make them quick. I knew right away there was never going to be any money coming from Randy. Right away, my first move was to let the manager know that we would be moving out at the end of that same month. I put up my furniture for sale as we now needed the cash. One by one, I sold the pieces of furniture. Randy dare not ask me for any money because, this time, I was completely annoyed, and I could be because he couldn't touch me. The question was where do I go from here because both Logan and Josh were in school.

My sister came to the rescue as she always did when I sought her help. Without a doubt, she agreed to take us in. By this stage, my sister had done well in life, completed her degree, and was now an assistant principal at a local elementary school. With that set in place, I got the apartment ready to be leased out as quickly as possible so that the penalty for breaking my lease would not be too great. Besides, I had to consider that as my stepdad had cosigned for me. By the grace of the Lord, it cost us $650 to get us out of the lease. The deposit I paid covered the rest of the expense. Again, my poor stepdad to the rescue. By this time, the money I owed my stepdad had accumulated to quite a large sum. But there was no talk of me returning any money to him, not yet anyway. Too much was going on for him to even ask me.

The day arrived when we had to move out. Getting a U-Haul rental, we packed the remaining items and headed for the storage unit near my sister's home. I still couldn't figure out how the kids were feeling about this whole situation. The plan was to keep the kids in their schools, and I transport them daily. I engaged the help of a consignment store to get rid of the remaining stuff I had in storage. I had put up advertisements on Craigslist. I needed to downsize the storage space as my sister willingly paid for it and continued to do so for the next year and a half. The plan was for us still to join Randy in South Africa.

Moving in with my sister was difficult as she had a two-bedroom apartment. My niece was still home with her, and my sister's new boyfriend at the time had just moved in with her too. In spite of this, my sister took me and the kids in. The new arrangement was Nicole and Logan shared the bedroom with my niece, while Josh and I slept in the living room. We had no idea how this event was going to change our lives—forever. I had no clue how my walk with the Lord was going to change my life. Randy had no clue how his life was going to be affected by these events either. As I struggled to settle into a routine, trying to keep things as normal for the kids as possible, life only got darker for me. The struggles became real, and I could see things spiraling downwards.

Our daily routine was getting up at five every day and driving Logan to the school bus stop at our old apartment. He got picked up at six fifteen, and then it was a wait in the car to seven thirty to drop off Josh who was now second grade. The many breakfasts being eaten in the car was a painful memory. Then back to my sister's apartment for the day, and then back to pick-up Josh at 1:50 p.m. only to drive to the bus stop to wait for Logan until 3:30 p.m. For months, this was my routine. During those trips, I listened to a Christian radio station every morning. It was so inspiring and uplifting.

However, depression was taking its toll on me. I spent the days reading the Word and talking to the Lord. Meditating on the book of Psalms gave me the strength to go from day to day. "The Lord shall preserve you from all evil, He shall preserve your soul" (Psalm 121). I would wake up in the middle of the night, restless, perturbed. I would go outside onto the patio to pray and talk to the Lord. Suddenly, my life was becoming an open book. I was scared, and I think, more embarrassed, to disclose some of the things that I was going through. Now an open book my life was becoming, but there were some things that just had to stay between me and my Jesus. He knew everything about me, and I felt secure with those things remaining with Him. I was now living under my sister's roof, and there were things and reasons I had to explain. Why else was I in this situation?

Here I was, left penniless, homeless with three children. My husband breaking all the promises he made to keep us safe and intact. I had no choice but to share things about my life. I looked needy and hopeless. Many nights, my sister's boyfriend found me on the patio on returning home from his midnight shift. I spent my time trying to reason with the Lord. The "why" questions asked over and over. How was I to know that the Lord was actually working and preparing me during this "why" season? I started my journal, documenting every thought and occurrence. Feelings were running high and low with no clue what the next day would bring. I had to trust in the Lord. In this time, I also took up writing poetry which I never knew I could do. Some of my best works, I would say!

For a few weeks, this transportation arrangement continued. All this back and forth started to take a toll on my already aging car. Nicole and Logan were beginning to experience their new freedom, but this enabled them to express their feelings. There was so much anger and, pretty soon, discord began to strain our relationship instead of building it up. Nicole started becoming agitated and rude and, sometimes, disrespectful in her attitude. It seemed that we have lived in turmoil for so long that we did not know how to live in peace. It was something I was afraid of as I chose that life because I let fear control me. Logan slipped into silent mode. I could not read him at all, and that concerned me. Randy has absconded all responsibilities as a father, and I was left to deal with all the attitudes the kids were giving me. He always said that they would take advantage of me if he was not around anymore. I hated the fact that this was now sounding true. It made me more angry. I was too wrapped up in my own emotional war to deal with this. Josiah just went with the flow of things. I must say, despite of what Nicole and Logan were feeling, they protected Josh from the trauma that was surrounding us.

The school year was drawing to a close, and I decided that Josh would switch schools. My sister was an assistant principal of a local elementary school and was able to enroll Josh in her school. This meant Josh would travel with my sister every day. One less task for me to do. Logan was entering high school, but his routine remained the same. I would transport him to the same bus stop near our old apartment.

Meanwhile, my mom's health had taken a turn for the worse. She showed up at my old apartment looking for me. Luckily, the manager knew my mom well and advised her that I had moved. She had forgotten that I moved away to my sister. Unbeknownst to us and my mom, the dementia was setting in and progressing very fast. Frustrated with herself for forgetting, she attempted to make her way to my sister's apartment—a trip that she so often made years before but now had no idea how to get there. She drove around for almost two hours and, finally, found her way back home in Miami. She called me later and was frantic about my whereabouts, and I reassured her that we were all well, and that her little Josh was safe. I did not know that she was attempting to pick him up from school like she normally did while we lived at our own place. She broke down because she could not find the school, and she became concerned that Josh was still waiting at the school. It was at this time my sister and I realized that the dementia had progressed so far that my mom would have to stop driving or going anywhere on her own. This was a sad day for us all.

My mom was an independent person, and she loved to drive. This meant no more trips to Georgia where they had a second home. Moving away from my old place took away the last and only job she had to keep her mind active. It broke my heart, and I felt solely responsible for my mom's condition. If only I could have stayed at my apartment longer, maybe the dementia would not have progressed so fast. If only I had not been burdened with all the decisions I had to make; if only I did not tell her about Randy's gambling problem; if only I did not tell her that I was leaving the States to go back to South Africa, my "Egypt"—so many questions, so much of guilt I carried. That day, my stepdad took away the keys for my mom's car. It broke his heart. He loved my mom so dearly. He was my mom's Boaz. He would do anything for her. All of this and God was shaping and molding us all, and we did not recognize any of this. Truly, God is the Potter, and we, certainly, are the clay in His hands.

CHAPTER 13

In the meantime, Randy's frustration began to rub off on me. Things were not working out as he thought it would. His brother had fired him from his only job. How could that be! His own brother? YES! Randy tried to double-cross his brother on a business deal that went south, and he was exposed. This meant no tickets to return to South Africa. I did not have the money, and neither did Randy. How can one person mess up so badly. Randy was given a simple assignment: go set up a place for us and get our tickets to return to South Africa.

Pressure began to build up. Now the argument took a different route. Before, I was to blame for coming to the States with no plan for the future; now the blame was wholly on his brother for splitting up his family. The relationship between Randy and his brother was severely strained. Bearing in mind, I still had to call Randy every day. Missing a day was reason for an explosive argument. How could someone 7,830 miles away make a person on the other line shiver with fear. Just hearing his angry voice would make my body tremble with fear. Randy was still controlling me even from that distance, and he knew it very well. Now I could have just hung up the phone instead of listening to all threats, but the thought never crossed my mind. I was so accustomed to accepting this behavior that I could not see there was a way out of this.

The summer vacation had begun, and my only income was from the sale of my items that I had in storage. Randy was pressuring me into getting the kid's passports in order while he tried to rack up the money to get us there. By this time, Nicole had made it clear she was never leaving the United States. Logan did not have a say in this matter because he was still a minor. All of these disruptions, and I was still willing to join Randy. Being a Christian wife, my place was with my husband. How misquoted I was! That was not according to the Word of God, not in my situation of domestic violence and abuse. But I remained faithful. Our temporary passports arrived during that summer, and now it was only a matter of getting the tickets. Somehow, Randy and his brother worked through their differences and made up; after all, they were brothers. So the promise streaks began again. The tickets would be ready this week, then next week, then end of the month. This went on from month to month.

With no financial support from Randy, it was difficult, yet my sister never once complained about having us with her. We lived as one family, loving and sharing everything. As the pressure built up, depression found a place in me. I refused to leave the apartment or socialize. Logan was spending much time with his best friend and his family—a family that took the place of our broken family. I did not realize that Logan was drifting away from me. Nicole was off, busy with her job and college classes. Poor Josh would sit in and watch television all day. Feeling like the whole world was crumbling on my head, I took to journalizing my feelings as I went along. Things just got darker and darker as the days went by, until I found myself staying in bed for days on end. I would wake up in the morning from the living floor bed and lay down in my niece's room. The kids were out most of the time. Josh and I slept in the bedroom when they were out.

One day, my sister had noticed that I had been in bed all day, and that caused her to be concerned. She knew if she did not force me out, there were going to be consequences and not good for me either. She tried her best and to no avail; I just refused. Dealing with Randy's tantrums and threats and now false accusations, my mind was about to blow. I remember waking up one morning and walking to the bathroom cabinet. There it was, staring me in the face—the solution to end this madness. I was exhausted, heartbroken, trapped—call it what it is when all hope is lost! As I reached for the deadly medication which I thought would be my answer to all this turmoil, I felt a sweet aroma sweep past my face, a warm sensation overcame my body. Paying no mind to this, I grabbed a bottle of water and emptied the bottle of pills into the palm of my hand. There it was again, a warm sensation tingling all over me. Just like a camera flash went on, I looked onto the mirror. What was I doing! This was not going to solve anything. What would become of Josiah, Logan and, of course, Nicole? Randy was doing what Randy does best—partying and having fun with no responsibility to bear but trying to keep me on the hook!

Just then, the sound of my sister's voice calling my name brought me back to reality. I hurriedly shoved the pills back into the bottle and replaced it in the bathroom cabinet. I was about to take my life, and that was totally against the Word of God. That night, I prayed asking God to forgive me for my selfishness, to give me the strength to go on. I delved deeper into His Word, making Him my foundation for all things (Psalm 69:14,15). My sister and I spent many nights talking about my situation. She had gotten to know some things about my life for the first time. Just talking to her, I felt like some of the burdens had been lifted. Keeping many things a secret for so many years, this was certainly liberating.

Summer passed and it was time for Logan and Josh to start school again. Back to the grind it was, driving Logan to the bus stop at 5:30 a.m. every morning. Josh was riding to school with my sister, but that meant he left home at 7:00 a.m. and returned at 6:00 p.m. daily. Long days for him, but it had to be done. The phone calls to Randy was diminishing slowly as I had to make choices: buy a phone card or put gas in my car. Unbeknownst to me, Randy was going from side job to side job, but no money was being earned, or so he said. Obviously, living at his mom's house, no bills, no support for me or the kids, he was free to do as he pleased. This was now beginning to make sense, and my eyes were being opened. Tired of being promised plane tickets from week to week, I decided to take another approach to things. With all threats during our phone conversations, I learnt to hang up the phone. I started to realize that he can't hurt me, physically, anyway. I had no reason to be so afraid of him. The strange thing was, Randy would swear that he loved me with all of his heart, and there was no one who could take my place. Back then, I was still very new to Facebook which became another way we stayed in contact. I used Facebook to keep Randy updated with the kids and their activities. They were beginning to miss him, from afar anyway.

Between shuttling Logan to and from the school bus stop, taking care of my sister's apartment, cooking meals, I was kept pretty occupied. My car was now showing signs of giving up on me. I did not have the money to have a mechanic to repair it. My stepdad was kind enough to repair it each time it failed on me. But it was now reaching a point beyond repair.

One day, I picked up Josh from school as my sister had a meeting to attend. As we got close to the apartment, I heard a clanking sound; no sooner, I saw smoke emerging from under the hood. In a panic, my first thought was the car was on fire as it was a fire hazard waiting to happen with all the repairs that were done. I had to get Josh out of the car! I put on the emergency hazard lights and pulled off to the side of the road, jumped out, and dashed to open the back door to get Josh out. He was strapped into the booster seat, and that was not one of the easiest things to unfasten quickly. This car could burst into flames any moment; I had to get my Josh out! Other motorists stopped to try to assist. Finally, I got Josh out of the car only to find out that the head gasket had blown. There was no moving that vehicle now.

We were still about a mile and a half away from the apartment. Our only option was to walk the rest of the way. It was still in the middle of summer, and this was a scorching day already. My time slot to call Randy had already passed, and I knew he would be furious because his jealous nature would have kicked in by this time. We had to pass a friend's house on the way, so I decided to stop and see if she was home. Maybe she would give us a ride as Josh was exhausted already. Luckily for us, she was home. So after explaining what had just happened to my car, I asked if I could use her phone to call

Randy. He did not hear anything I said of what we just experienced. His first angry response was why I was late in calling him, and why was I making Josh walk in the heat! Filled with embarrassment as my friend had overheard him yelling and cursing at me, I hung up the phone. Kindly, she offered us a ride home. She told me not to worry about the car, that she will have her husband and son tow it back to the apartment later that evening. Thanking her for her assistance, she hugged us, and feeling a deep sympathy, she left. Later that evening, my car was towed to the apartment.

I was now without transport. I still needed to get Logan to the bus stop the next day. The *grace* of God I call it. My sister's boyfriend offered to let me use his spare car. I was able to fulfill my daily routine. Randy still had not sent any money to help us get through with the daily expenses. I guess he thought being with my sister made things all right. My cash flow was running low, so the next alternative was to sell my car to the junk yard, which I did, and managed to rack up another three hundred dollars. Praise the Lord. Obtaining tickets now seemed far-fetched. I was growing tired of Randy and his brother making promises to get us over and nothing came close.

As Christmas approached, we were no further from where we had started in May of that year. Randy had got involved with heavy gambling and had started drinking again. Thank God that I did not have to endure being in his presence during those times. We were safe for now. Excuses is all I got from Randy when I asked for any assistance from him. I was just wasting my time.

As I got deeper into the Word of God, I began to see the Scriptures in a different way. I read them before, but now, they took on different meaning. The mist was clearing up in my head. I began to feel and enjoy the real peace. I started exercising and becoming more active. I was still unable to work as there was no change in my immigration status. I occupied myself with many projects in the day.

By this time, I was growing tired of the cat-and-mouse game with the tickets for travel. I had begun to hear about Randy and his explicit ventures. He was making no attempt to get us down there. He was always full of excuses every time we spoke. Yet for some crazy reason, I did not think of the option of staying in the United States and continuing my life here without him. I was still set on joining him at some point. Against the wishes of my family, I still was set to go.

Two days before Christmas, I got a call from Randy's sister. She was aware of our situation here, and she was also very well aware of Randy's vague attempts of getting us to South Africa any time soon. She had managed to get some money from him and was going to wire it for the kid's Christmas. I was so appreciative for her compassion. Randy continued on, what I called, his party streak. It seemed he had grown comfortable with his surroundings, and it didn't matter when we got there, but he was so sure that someday we would be together. That was certainly no way to live life. This was a one-sided affair. Here I was, struggling to survive with three kids, no home of our own, and almost penniless. He shared no responsibility with the kids at all. It was all on me, fixing his mess again.

As the holidays passed, and we came into the new year, my mind got clearer. I started to see a glimpse of new hope. The peace of us being away from direct contact with Randy was settling in. Although we were struggling to make a life, peace and laughter were slowly returning to our lives. Nicole and Logan started feeling more at ease—not comfortable but at ease.

By this time, Randy was unemployed again, living off his mother. I could only assume he did not care because it was now almost closing on to one year, and there were no changes in him. The thing that upset me the most was he seemed comfortable with the idea that we had a place to stay, and he did not have to support us. I believe, as a husband and father, you would cross the seas or climb the highest mountain to ensure that your family is taken care of by you, not relying on other people to do it for you. This was not Randy's case, and it seemed, he was satisfied with this.

My sister continued to pursue me and encouraged me to keep my head up, and she said she believed in me that I would survive this. At the same time, my brother, who was more like a parent to me growing up because my mom left me with him when she immigrated to the United States, shut down my decision about returning to South Africa. It was not a suggestion but a command that I remain in the US. My prayer warrior aunt and amazing sister-in-law put a sizable amount of cash together, along with my brother, who was willing to do whatever he had to do to ensure I could get a head start and make a new life here.

As I sought the Lord in my daily meditation and as I journalized my days, the clouds in my life began to slowly clear. Randy made all kinds of excuses to his friends back in South Africa for the reasons his family had not yet arrived. Lies led to bigger lies, and soon, everything he said was fabricated. He gave the impression that we were living rather extravagant lives here, and I remained behind to take care of all the businesses we supposedly had. About the same time, I found out that Randy and his brother always had plans to have Josh accompany Randy to South Africa. In planning this, it was one sure way that I would never fall back on not joining him. But the Lord unknowingly protected me from that. On hearing all of this, it disgusted me. How cruel! The first chance I got, I related the truth to his sister of how he left us here, homeless and penniless. I was not looking for compassion from her, but his family also needed to know the truth about him or, at least, face up to the reality that he wasn't what he appeared to be.

My forty-sixth birthday was coming up, and I was starting to come out of my shell of depression and hopelessness. My sister always made all of our birthdays a special occasion. She came home that evening with a small cake, and we celebrated over a glass of wine. That weekend, we were invited to join one of my sister's friend and her husband on a boat trip on the Intracoastal of Fort Lauderdale. I had no clue how my life was about to be impacted with this trip.

I remember waking up that Saturday morning, excited. This was a day that the Lord had made, and I was going to rejoice in it no matter what came my way! Being on the boat on the open water that beautiful cool morning was like a breath of fresh air that I was breathing for the first time. I felt like nothing else mattered. I felt the freedom like I never felt before. My sister's friends were the sweetest couple ever. They knew I was going through a very difficult time in my life and felt this trip would release some of the pressure, but they did not know what a life-changing moment this was going to be for me and my children.

As we took to the open water, Lance, our boat captain, took advantage of taking us on a short but top-speed ride. I felt like Kate Winslet on the bow of the Titanic. There was no Leonardo Di Caprio, but here I was, feeling the freedom of life for the very first time. As the cool breeze blew my hair back and over my face, I stretched out my arms to feel the wind. I felt like I was flying high in the sky, and nothing could touch me there—no yelling, no violence, no threats, no fear, no lies, no more tearing down of my self-esteem. I was my own woman at last! If I may say, I think the sea breeze blew sense into my brain that day! What a wonderful experience and day that was.

As we were approaching the dock, I suddenly realized what I had to do! This is where my life was! Why on earth would I want to go to a place where I would be imprisoned again, stripped of all confidence and, most of all, my womanhood? There was no way I was going back to my "Egypt" to be a slave! God was opening my Red Sea; the choice to cross was mine to make, mine only. God's handwriting was all over this day and over me! And then I said it, "I am not going back!" Shouting at the top of my voice, I repeated this, "I am not going back!" just so I heard myself too, loud and clear. My sister and her friends looked at me, and their faces lit up.

With tears in her eyes, my sister turned around and hugged me and said, "I knew you would come to your senses!"

That day, I realized, taking a leap of faith is like jumping off a cliff. You will find your wings on the way down, and God will lift you up to soar the heights you have never seen before. All you have to do is trust Him! We went home that night, and I shared with Nicole and Logan my decision. The relief on their faces, the hugs, the tears, followed. The fears, heartbreaks, lies, secrets were over.

My first task was to find a job. My entire life now rested in the arms of the Lord. As I embarked on a project to help renovate my sister's kitchen, I came into contact with the maintenance staff of the apartment building. As we chatted, I found out that there was to be a vacant apartment for lease on the ground floor. I arranged to meet with the owner a few days later to view the apartment. Mind you, I had no job at this time, but I was going to look at this apartment with the possibility of leasing it. Looking at the view of the golf course from the living room was breathtaking. The nights I had spent on my sister's patio praying and dreaming of my own place seemed within reach. I know with God all things are possible! And this was one of the first. The owner was pleasant and willing to help anyway he could. I told him that I can only afford seven hundred dollars a month. So we agreed, finally, and if I was to get a job within the next two weeks, the apartment would be mine. Total favor of God was upon us.

Networking through some friends, I managed to land a job. I was going to use my niece's identification because we looked so much alike, and I needed this job. I knew this was not the right thing to do, but I had to trust that God was going to favor me. Waiting tables for the first time was a challenge at first, but soon, it became a breeze. Not long, I started to find the real me. I was not this shy, low-esteemed, introverted person that was displayed for so many years. I had a vibrant personality which was waiting to be explored. Soon, I became the popular girl among the customers, and the owners really grew to love me. I worked very hard and diligently.

Within two weeks, we were able to move into our apartment on the ground floor. My brother had helped with the security deposit. The items left in storage was sufficient to get us off the ground. I still remember the reaction of the kids when they walked into the empty apartment that day. Rolling on the carpeted floor, so excited, they did not even mind that the place would be unfurnished for a while, but this was our own. Nicole and Logan moved the stuff from the storage into the apartment while I had to go to work. Coming to the apartment later that evening was glorious. A place we can finally call home!

A week later, with the rest of the money my brother had sent, I was able to get mattress sets for us all and, praise be to God, a minivan. My sister's boyfriend was kind enough to insure the vehicle with his insurance agent; my license, by the grace of God, still had two years before it would expire. All of this could only be the hands of God over us. The most hilarious thing was obtaining a telephone service in the apartment. I did not have a cell phone and could not really afford one right then as there were other priorities. So we used one of the remote telephones with the base and placed in a spot where it would receive the signal from my sister's apartment upstairs. The cable services were already set up by the owner. Grace from the Lord was written all over this. And so, we began our new lives.

CHAPTER 14

In the meantime, my phone calls to Randy had diminished to maybe once a month. When he did speak to the kids, his conversation would be interrogating about my activities instead of trying to reconnect with them. They still very much respected him as their father, but these conversations were not beneficial, and they saw it as him not caring about their well-being but rather, curious about my life and what I was doing now that he was not around me. He appeared rather disrespectful most of the time, and both Nicole and Logan did not appreciate his disrespect for me. He even tried to question little Josh about me, and that caused even more confusion in his mind.

It had been months since we had seen my mom. Dementia was now in a full-blown stage. It was a tough time for us all, dealing with my mom's condition and trying to balance my life.

I had heard through the grapevines that he was back to his old tricks—drinking, gambling, partying, with which came the womanizing. Surprisingly, I did not care for it. My freedom and peace meant more to me, besides, the children were happy with our new life. We kept in touch via Facebook. I remained pleasant to him. I never disclosed to him that we now had our own place, and that I was working. But somehow, he found out later that I had started work. He was keeping in touch with some of his old friends here, and I suppose, one of them may have told him. His friends had no knowledge of all the things he had put us through. He always played the perfect husband and father while in their presence. But now, I was aware that he was trying to keep tabs on me through his friends. With this in place, suddenly, his plans changed. His family was trying to get him shipped back to the United States. I knew they would soon get tired of him and try push him off on us again. There was no way I was going to let him get off that easily. No way I was going to let him back into our lives. I had made that dreadful mistake before and paid dearly for those consequences. Things had to change. Change could not be with Randy back in our lives.

Yet, I still thought I would test his integrity. He was trying to obtain another visa to come back to the United States, so I told him to send me the one thousand dollars which would be the penalty for overstaying his first visa, and he could then apply for a new one. His response was strike one for my case for any reconciliation in our marriage. His response was, "Now that you are working, you can work your butt off and pay the penalty!" I would have to be out of my mind to do any such thing. Support three children plus a household to run, and now him! No way!

A few days later, a frantic call from his niece put another piece of the puzzle together for his family to learn more about him. Randy, apparently, was trying to borrow a large sum of money from his niece, and she was trying to ascertain if she should lend him the money. This was my chance to set some things straight. Should she desire to go ahead, there was no way she would get paid back, and I certainly was in no position to do so either. She had no idea of the condition he left us in when he came to South Africa. This was all news to her, and she expressed her sorrows, but she was glad that we were getting on our feet again.

It was weeks since I had spoken to Randy, and I felt good. He sent several messages through Facebook wanting me to call him. I did not respond. Call it intuition, but I decided to check up on his Facebook messages. And there it was—my answer to bring this case to a close—a detailed message to one of his ex-girlfriends, expressing his regret marrying me, and how sorry he was for mistreating her while we were dating each other, how he should have listened to his mother and married her, how much he loved her and how he missed her and he wanted so much to reconnect with her, and so on and so on. Hmm, lots of food for thought

After much thought, I decided to sit Nicole and Logan down and let them know the decision I was about to make. I did not want then to hold me responsible for this family breaking up, besides, Randy was still their father. I had to make sure that all things were clear. And then I showed them the message from Facebook which I printed out should I have needed it as proof later on. Both Nicole and Logan, despite all they had been through, were so disappointed and hurt that their own father would deny them as his children and the fact that he regretted everything about us. They both were so appreciative that I would trust them with confidential information, and it also made them feel part of me.

I spent the next few days seeking the wisdom of the Lord. I did not share this incident with anybody else. My life being an open book already was enough. This had to end, and end now! I came home one afternoon after work and decided to put an end to all this drama. Hearing Randy's voice on the other end of the line was the test I needed to pass, and I did! I did not feel an ounce of fear for him. My thoughts were, *He can't hurt me anymore!* Listening to him trying to ply me with love and affection only infuriated me, but I kept my composure, waiting for the right moment.

And then I seized my chance! It was like I was taken to another dimension. This was not in my character to be demanding or even taking charge. Now was the time, and I let him have it! The words started off calm and softly as they proceeded from my mouth to Randy's ears that day, "Listen up, Randy, I want you to shut your mouth and listen to what I have to say. Don't breathe, don't do anything, just shut up and listen!" I reiterated his entire Facebook message to him. If only I could have seen the look on his face when I did, that would have been priceless for all the years of terror he had put me through.

He sounded like a puppy with his tail between his legs trying to make excuses, that he did not mean any of those things he wrote as he recorded it as, "When someone is under pressure, people say things that they don't mean!" He didn't mean to say them, that he loved me only with all his heart, and the children were so precious to him.

Not giving him the time of day to make any more excuses, I said these final words before hanging up, "I am done with you! Did you hear me, I'm done!" I yelled so loudly through the entire conversation that my throat hurt so bad, but I never felt so good in my life! After thirty-three years, I finally got my moment, and all glory to my God for giving me the strength to endure and persevere through all those years. I was finally done with my "Egypt." I chose to remain, by faith, in my "land of milk and honey."

I continued to work very hard, pulling double shifts where I could. By this time, I was fully managing and waiting tables at the restaurant. I saw a new side to life, one I could enjoy without fear or intimidation. From weighing a whopping one hundred and fifty-six pounds, I suddenly weighed one hundred and twenty! My new hair color and style made me feel amazing. For the first time, I was able to focus on me. Take care of me! I did become the new attraction at my workplace. For the first time, I felt like a real woman. I enjoyed the attention I was getting, but I knew my boundaries. I mean, I was able to pass for being twenty-seven years of age at the age of forty-five, which was my secret! Oh, how good it felt! It seemed like the Lord had come full circle for me, but I had no idea that He was just getting started with me.

Time passed. Then came a day the phone rang at the restaurant. I answered as usual, and heard a voice that sounded all too familiar. I felt a cold shiver run down my spine. It was Randy! How he had come to know exactly where I worked was a shock to me. And the yelling began. I just hung up the phone. Shaken from hearing his angry voice, it stirred up old feelings again. Moments later, the phone rang again. I picked up and, trying to keep calm, told him not to call me at my place of work, but as usual, the threats began. Now Randy was a smart guy, a very smart guy. He kind of figured out my plan for being able to get a job at the restaurant and assuming that is what I did, he used this as leverage to threaten me—threaten he would expose me! And he sure did try. I explained to the owner my situation, and he was so compassionate toward me. He told me not to worry about anything, that he will take care of this issue. So the next day, the owner answered Randy's call. Randy, being the coward that he was, told the owner that I was a fraud and was working under an assumed name. He tried his best, but the owner threatened to put the authorities onto him if he did not stop these harassing calls. He informed him at the same time that I no longer worked there. Now what kind of man would want to see his own children go hungry? My income was the only source keeping a roof over his children and putting food on the table. Was he that selfish or was it desperation? I had to trust that *my* Lord would work out the details and the job would not be in jeopardy. Randy tried again a few weeks later, and he was told the same thing. Thank God for caller ID, I was able to know when he was calling in so I got one of my coworkers to answer, and the owner had briefed them on what to say. Eventually, he stopped calling at the restaurant. In the interim, he was also calling Josh's school demanding to speak with him. My sister had notified the office staff briefly about the situation, and he was told that no student was allowed phone calls. Randy had the craziest thoughts. He held my sister responsible for our marriage breaking up. He blamed her for influencing my decision to end our marriage or, rather, this reign of terror, as I saw it. Not once did he see himself as the reason for this break up. To him, he was blameless, and he was the victim of circumstances. Truly the thoughts and actions of a deranged person, I would say. However, it was not my job to judge him or anybody for that matter but the Lord's. After a few more attempts at calling Josh's school, Randy stopped. We kept a low profile so as to avoid any further issues.

Life was wonderful. The kids were happy. That was all that mattered to me. The lost years of my youth, my young adult life and, later, my adult life, I had to try to make up for lost time. I really was beginning to blossom. The real me finally got the chance to be explored. I drew up a bucket list of things I wanted to accomplish. Sounds silly, but enjoying my newfound social life was an amazing experience. Coming home and not having to answer to anyone but to God and myself was a priceless feeling. The peace we had was astounding. I did not know how I was going to fix my immigration status. I did not know what each day would bring. I did not know how I will renew my driver's license when it was up for renewal which was a necessity. All I was focused on was my Jesus and stayed before him in obedience. He was now my only hope to survive in this country. But I was not about to let anything steal my joy. For too many years, I allowed the enemy to rob me and destroy everything I had. My job now was to focus on the LORD—and I trusted that HE would do the rest—and to keep taking the steps of faith as He led me down this new journey.

And then it happened, September 9, 2012, one Sunday afternoon. After pulling a double shift at the restaurant the night before and just finishing my day shift, these were words from a total stranger as he shook my hand to greet me, "Your life is about to change! Do you mind if I pray with you?"

Little did I know that the story of Ruth and Boaz from the Book of Ruth was about to be reenacted, but this time, in my era, to become *my story*!

A fairy tale, every girl's dream was about to come to life, and I was going to be the *princess* of my own *story*.

CPSIA information can be obtained
at www.ICGtesting.com
Printed in the USA
BVHW031623071019
560429BV00004B/389/P